Reviews

"Fish Tails - Bones Not Included" by Mark T. Bradbury is just what I needed . . . a vacation. It took me back to my early days of fishing. As an enthusiastic novice, hungry for knowledge, tips and tricks I gorged myself on every word written by the established experts who had come before me. Fish Tails was just like reading the outdoor magazines that I devoured as a youngster - anecdotes, adventure, technique, and philosophy all rolled into a well-conceived anthology. This collection of stories chronicles Mark's evolution as an angler and expresses how fishing is more than just a sport or skill necessary to catch a fish.

Bradbury's style is free and easy. He can cover a lot of ground in a short distance on the page with his descriptions of places, people, situations and feelings. Like the old outdoor writers, he puts you in the middle of the action and leaves you with a longing to participate as soon as possible in creating your own memories. There is concern for the resource of the fisheries, practices and habitat that weaves its way into the heart of the reader so that fishing will still be possible for generations to come.

Chip Curry – Artist, Writer, Blogger

Every true fisherman remembers their first catch. Bradbury takes the reader on an anecdotal journey through the life stories of an avid angler.

With an easy style that takes you from that first experience through the many others to follow, the author's recounts of the adventures (and the misadventures everyone who has ever fished can relate to) of a lifelong passion of piscatorial pursuit.

They're told in a style that makes you think it was your buddy standing next to you, chest-deep in the river, as you both cast your lines and fill time until you feel the tug of the prey.

Go ahead and take a nibble. I'll bet you swallow the bait!

David Higgins – Deerfield Beach, FL

Fish Tails –
Bones Not Included

An Angler's Look at Life

MARK T. BRADBURY

little pond
publishing
littlepondpublishing.com

Fish Tails –
Bones Not Included

By Mark T. Bradbury
Website address: mtbradbury1.blogspot.com

Copyright © 2014 by Mark T. Bradbury
ISBN: 978-1-940720-10-4
First Published 2014 Printed in the United States of America
First Printed 2014
Originally published by Little Pond Publishing, Inc
Cover Design and Book Production by Karen I. Smith

From the Author

It's often been said that one's life is the sum of his experiences. It might be true, but that's a bit too deep for me, since philosophy never was my most gifted arena of study. Let's keep it simple, sir, or the K.I.S.S. Theory, has been my model of choice as much as possible.

And so, the only things deep we're going to talk about in the following chapters are about water, as in deep water, fresh or salty. That's as deep as it'll get. This is a book about fishing, and if you've been fishing, you know that it beats the hell out of anything philosophical. We've all seen the bumper sticker that boldly proclaims "A bad day of fishing beats a great day at work!" That's my kind of philosophy, as good as it gets, and I salute the person who's immortalized the phrase for all of us!

If you've been fishing for more than a week or two, then you might have some better stories than you'll read here. That's your story to write; I'm just telling mine. Some poetic license may be in abundance in the pages beyond, but this is a book of fish stories, and who hasn't stretched the truth about the big one that got away (always gets away). Enjoy them, have fun and keep your lines wet!

Fish on! Screaming drags to all of you!

The Neighbor

It was 1961, and life was pretty simple. My parents had bought a house in the country in a small Massachusetts town called Dighton. Dighton seemed like it was a million miles from anything I had previously experienced, but I soon learned that there were all sorts of things to discover there.

There was a half mile of trees behind our house, and in the middle of the woods there was a series of small ponds. The locals called them peat bogs, whatever that meant. The ponds froze over in the winter, and the local kids would skate all day long out there. I always used to think that these ponds must be filled with some big fish, but having no real knowledge of fishing, that assumption had gone unanswered.

The following spring our neighbor, Mr. Lounsbury, was out in his driveway with quite an assortment of fishing gear. He seemed to be cleaning and organizing a bunch of fishing rods and tackle in the back of his big station wagon. Mr. Lounsbury had a reputation for being an old grouch to all the kids, and many of the adults, in our neighborhood, but showing no fear I approached him as he worked. I very gingerly cleared my throat and barely whispered "Mr. Lounsbury, is that all your fishing stuff?"

He hadn't heard or seen me coming up on him, and it startled him a bit. He turned on me quickly, and I expected the worst. Fearing that he was about to scream at me and chase me out of his yard, he surprised me when he stopped and sized me up without saying a word. Finally, after a few seconds that felt like an hour, he actually spoke.

"Yeah, kid, it is. At least most of it; I've got more in the cellar, but I only use that if I go saltwater fishing. You that new kid from next door at the Gramm's old place?"

"Yes sir, I am. My name's Mark."

"You like to fish, kid?"

"I'm not sure, Mr. Lounsbury. My dad doesn't fish, so I haven't had any chances. But I think it looks like fun; I've read a lot of stories in *Outdoor Life*."

A warm smile slowly developed on the face of the *old grouch*. He started to chuckle a bit, and told me to sit down on his picnic table. "Fishing is more fun than you can even imagine, but you'll have times when you think it's the cruelest thing you could ever do to yourself.

I've been fishing since my grandfather took me out to his farm pond when I was much younger than you. We used long cane poles made out of bamboo from China; he put a big, fat garden worm on the hook and just threw out the line as far as it would go. He attached a bobber on the line so we'd know when we had a bite.

He poured us some lemonade my grandmother made for us, but I had barely taken a sip when the bobber on my line started going crazy. He jumped up, moving faster than I'd ever seen him move, and grabbed my pole. He yanked back on it, and I saw the pole bending over. Then he handed it to me, and told me to let the fish run around a bit until it got tired. When my hands went around that big cane pole my whole body got a jolt. I was so excited I almost stepped into the pond.

I let that fish run around for a few minutes, and at my grandfather's urging, I started to pull it in towards the bank. When it got close to the cattails near the shore it got a second wind, and started running away from me. My grandfather told me not to pull too hard, but to keep the line tight. I kept it tight, thinking the whole time that I was probably going to take the fish's head off in the process.

Before that happened, I started to sense that I was in control. The fish on the end of my line was getting tired, and I could tell it would be over soon. I could do this, I knew, but I had to be strong. I worked the fish back toward me, and this time as it approached the cattails, I held the line as tight as I could. I pulled the fish right up onto the bank, and my grandfather got his trousers wet right up to his knees helping me land my prize."

"Good lord, you caught a bass! Must be two to three pounds!" my grandfather cried out, more excited than I had ever seen him! "Congratulations, son, you're an *official* fisherman. I brought you out here thinking we'd catch some calicoes or sunfish, but you got the real deal. What a nice fish!"

"My bass was green and black, with a large mouth. My hook and worm were caught on the corner of that big mouth, and I thought to myself that was one pretty fish. At the time I didn't know a bass from a goldfish, but my grandfather's proclamation was right; I've been a fisherman ever since!"

Sitting and listening to his story without saying a word, I jumped up as excited as he probably was back then. I knew right there that becoming an "official" fisherman was within my grasp; a rod and reel were all that was necessary. It turned out that Mr. Lounsbury was not only an accomplished angler, but he knew how to hook more than fish. I had taken the bait and swallowed the hook; I was sold.

Gearing Up

After the encounter with Mr. Lounsbury, I went home and told my Dad his story. Learning how to fish was my goal, and Mr. Lounsbury could help me with that. We went down to the cellar and he pulled out some fishing rods that were stuck up in the rafters. It turned out that he had done some fishing when I was very young, but had given it up years before. The gear had been collecting dust up until then, but would soon find new life. It was time to fish!

I headed over to Mr. Lounsbury's house with my newly found equipment. He was still out in the yard, sitting at the picnic table, playing with one of his beagles. The little dog barked, but her tail wagged as I bent over to give her the mandatory head scratch. Everything was good once that was out of the way.

Seeing me carrying a fishing rod and reel, Mr. Lounsbury called out to me. "Whatcha got there? Looks like you're ready to go."

"Yes sir, I am. My Dad had this stuff down in the cellar; I didn't even realize what it was until he took it down for me. He told me I can 'borrow' it for now, until I get my own gear. I've got a great paper route, and I mow the Turner's and Silva's lawns every week. I should be able to save up some money real soon, then I can buy a new spinning rod and reel like you've got. Do you suppose you can help me get started? I don't know anything about fishing, or even how to cast this pole. I could sure use the help. Maybe I can cut your grass, or rake some leaves, or something else you need done here. I'm not afraid to work, sir."

He started laughing at me again. The words had spilled out of me in a blur, and he thought it was quite comical. Not caring if he laughed, I patiently awaited his answer.

When he stopped laughing he told me that he thought I might show up asking for help. "What did you think, I was going to get you all excited, and not help you?"

Taking a deep breath, I knew that it was only a short time before my fishing dreams would become fishing stories. Thanking him, probably ten times, I went on to ask when we could start.

"How about Saturday afternoon? I'm heading down to Cape Cod to do some trout fishing on Friday night. I usually stay overnight and head home a couple hours after sunrise. I take a nap when I get home, so I'll yell over to you when I'm ready to get started. Bring your rod and reel; if you have some extra money right now, I'll give you a list of things you can pick up before Saturday. It's some basic tackle that I use that I'll show you how to fish with."

"That'll be great! I already have twenty dollars saved up, so what should I get?"

"Let me get a pencil and pad to write it down. Be right back."

He was back in a few minutes carrying a large tackle box along with the pencil and paper he'd gone in for. He started pulling things out of his box, telling me what each item was; hooks, swivels, sinkers, split shot, rubber worms, Rebels, bobbers and different sized monofilament lines. "These are my tools of the trade, as they say. Most of the bass and trout I catch are caught with one or more of these things. If you get this stuff before Saturday, I'll show you how to get started."

"Super! I'll get as much as I can; this'll be great!"

He went on to describe each item he had removed from his tackle box. He showed me assorted sizes of hooks, explaining that every fish required a different one. He told me to buy the shiny gold ones because they were a better quality, and went on to tell me a bit about each one. He did the same for the swivels, sinkers and such, and then got to the rubber worms and Rebels. He said that it was imperative that I buy the same worms he had, at the same store. He claimed that they were the truest imitation, and they worked better than anything he had ever fished with.

He told me to buy a black and silver Rebel if there was enough money left over, in the medium size. Pulling one from his box, he told me it could be my best friend sometime when nothing else was working. The Rebel was a hard plastic small fish imitation, with two sets of triple (or treble, as he called them) hooks attached to the body. It had a clear plastic tongue extending from the front of its mouth. He told me that it wasn't supposed to be a tongue; it just made the bait swim in a back and forth motion that drove fish wild. He promised to show me how to use it when we were out fishing.

The list was complete, and I couldn't wait to get downtown to buy my tackle. My dad gave me a ride to the big hardware store on Main St. the next day, the store he told me to go to. Buying everything he instructed me to buy, including the silver and black Rebel, we went up to the checkout counter. My twenty dollars was in my pocket; it was an assortment of dollar bills and change, all earned doing lawns, delivering newspapers and shoveling snow in the winter. As the clerk tallied my gear on the cash register, I eagerly awaited the total. Not knowing how much everything added up to, I was a bit apprehensive.

"That'll be $18.53, with the tax."

I exhaled and pulled my money from the pocket of my old Wrangler jeans. Being twelve years old and making my first purchase of fishing tackle was exciting, almost exhilarating, and I couldn't believe I was on my way to catching a fish. Little did I know then that the pile of dollar bills and loose change sitting on the counter of the old sporting goods store would be my first installment of a lifetime of money spent chasing fish. But if I didn't spend it, there wouldn't be any stories to tell, would there?

Basic Training

Saturday morning was the day to mow the neighbors' lawns. I got up early, gassed up the mower and got started. It usually took about two hours to do both yards, but I was flying the whole time. I completed them in less than an hour and a half, giving me hours to get ready for my lesson later that day. My Dad had given me an old Army knapsack to put my tackle into, and I took my newly purchased gear out of that bag at least a dozen times, checking to make sure that everything Mr. Lounsbury had told me to get was still there. Despite confirming each time that it was, the nervous energy pouring through me kept me doing it over and over.

His Chevy station wagon was in his driveway, so I knew he was home. I had seen him drive by when I was mowing the lawns across the street, but how long his nap would take was the big question. Time dragged by; my mother had called me in for lunch and I could hardly eat. My nerves were jangling; I needed to get started.

I finally heard his voice calling across the field between our houses. It was a little after two o'clock, and he was ready to have me come over. I grabbed my bag of tackle and my rod and reel, and ran up the short path between our houses. We were about to start what would become a lifelong journey for me, and I couldn't wait!

He was already sitting at the picnic table when I pulled up and deposited my bag of goodies. I poured them out all over the table, and waited for his approval. He checked it all out, noting that I had indeed bought every single thing he told me to. "Looks like you got what we need to get started. I think we'll work on tying a basic fishing knot on mono-filament first, and then we'll work on some of these other things. We'll string some worms and tie some leaders, and then we'll see how well you can cast that rod. How does that sound?"

"Whatever you want to do, Mr. Lounsbury. There's a lot to learn, so let's get started!"

He knew it was crazy to put me off any longer, so he grabbed my rod and pulled off a length of line, handing it to me. He grabbed one of the shiny hooks and handed it to me. "Go ahead and show me what you think is a good fishing knot."

Stringing the end of the line through the eye of the hook, I looped it around and tied a perfect *square knot*, something I had learned back in Boy Scouts. It wasn't perfect; there was a piece of leftover line about a half inch long dangling off the end of my knot.

He was smiling as he took the hook in his hand, telling me to hold on to the rod. He tugged on the hook, and it broke free from the line immediately. Monofilament line wasn't rope; the square knot was useless, and I was pretty bummed out about failing my first test.

"Hey, don't worry about that. Everybody makes that mistake. Mono line is as slippery as anything, and tying a knot that holds is one of the most important things you'll need to know. Let's show you how to tie a fishing knot; here, give me your rod and watch what I do."

He took the rod, released some line from the reel and

threaded the line through a hook. He looped it around about six times, and then ran the line back through the space left open. He threaded it back one more time through the remaining loop and pulled it tight. He pulled out a pair of nail clippers and snipped the leftover line close to the knot, announcing as he finished that it was what was known as a fisherman's knot. Today we know it as the *improved clinch knot*; I've probably tied it about a million times in my life.

We worked on the fisherman's knot for quite a while, until I was confident of doing it in the dark. He had told me that I would probably tie more knots in near or full darkness than in broad daylight, so I listened and tied it until it was second nature. The words of wisdom concerning tying knots in the dark was as prophetic as anything else he taught me; as we all know, that's when many of the world's game fish hunt, and that's when we hunt them.

A good part of the afternoon was spent tying leaders and stringing rubber worms. I remember thinking that day the idea of fish chasing a plastic worm instead of a fat, juicy night crawler was as crazy as I ever heard, but my mentor was telling me they worked, and challenging his knowledge wasn't in the cards. We also worked on casting my Dad's rod, which had an open-faced spinning reel. It was an earlier version of what Mr. Lounsbury used, but the technique was the same. Like every beginner, I held it upside down at first, thinking that it was the only thing that made any sense. Oops, another strike! Everything I thought I knew coming in had gone up in smoke before my eyes.

It was around five o'clock when he determined that we had done enough for the day. I was disappointed that my lessons were over, but he brought a smile back to my face when he asked if I'd like to go fishing tomorrow evening after dinner. Of course I jumped on the chance and declared myself ready to go.

Thinking back to all the times I had thought about the big fish lurking in the depths of the peat bogs behind our house I suggested that we try there. He broke into a wide grin, and proceeded to tell me that the only things swimming around in the bogs were some tadpoles and turtles. Not a good start for me; that was *Strike 3!*

He told me we'd be fishing in the mill pond behind the old textile factory a half mile away. The defunct mill had once been one of hundreds of textile factories scattered across New England, but tough times had forced the mills to close up and move south to the Carolinas. Their legacy was a tremendous availability of industrial space and some incredible dammed-up reservoirs, full of fish and wildlife. That's where my obsession began.

The Dam

Mr. Lounsbury had told me to come over around six o'clock. Of course I was in his driveway at 5:45, camped out next to his '58 Chevy station wagon. He must have expected me to be early, because he walked out and told me to put my gear in the back of the car. I opened the back door and saw his rods and tackle already stacked in there. Within minutes, we were on the way to what he liked to call his *honey hole*. He went past the old mill and took a left down a dirt road heading west. It was part of the property once owned by the textile company, and was open to the public for access to the pond. The pond was about two miles long at its northern point before turning back into the river that fed the reservoir, and he told me that the dirt road ran along most of the pond's length, offering lots of places to fish along its banks.

But his favorite spot was right at the original old dam behind the mill. The water moved pretty well there, and there was lots of forage for the fish that came here every night. He parked the car in a clearing just off the road and shut it down. We both jumped out and grabbed our rods and tackle.

There was a path worn through the woods heading towards the dam. He told me it was an old Indian trail that followed the original river out to the biggest watershed in our area, the Taunton River. The Taunton River flowed into the ocean south of Dighton, so this path had actually been a small highway to the ocean for the Native Americans who lived here hundreds of years before.

We arrived at the dam. It was about seventy-five yards across, with four foot high retaining walls at each end. Standing on the north wall, looking out over the water, we saw swirls and pops in different spots; he told me that was good, since it was a sign that the fish were here.

He took out one of the *rubber worms* we had rigged the day before, and had me tie it onto my line. After completing a perfect knot, he reminded me to make sure that my bail was open when casting. He saw a big swirl off to our left close to the dam and told me to cast over there as close as I could. "Pop it around a little bit as soon as it lands in the water" he said.

I put three casts right over the edge of the dam, watching as they flew down the spillway. I retrieved my wayward casts as quickly as possible, but by the time I got a clean cast near the big swirl the fish had moved out. Mr. Lounsbury had been casting over to the right with his own rubber worm as he watched my worm repeatedly fly over the dam. He smiled, but never said a word. He just told me to keep trying, and he kept fishing.

While practicing my ineptitude, I heard a loud splash and a zinging noise coming from my right. My tutor had something hooked that was swimming all over the place. He asked me not to cast anymore, and to take my line out of the water. His fish was trying to bury itself in the lily pads about a hundred feet out. He kept his line tight, rod bending, and kept reeling in line whenever the fish gave him some slack. I grabbed the long-handled net that he had brought along, and stood off to the side prepared to help, waiting for the right moment.

He saw me with the net and asked if I ever used one before. He was just being polite, because for sure he knew it was as foreign to me as rocket propulsion. I told him no, but the fish was getting in close now and he needed my help. "Go ahead! Get the net right under him and lift it up quickly."

How hard could this be, I thought. I went to the side of the wall, struck my pose and waited as he brought the fish up to me. Suddenly the fish was right in front of me; it was big, and it was staring right at me. I froze.

"Quick! Do it now!"

Taking a step forward, I dipped the net into the water below the fish, quickly bringing it up out of the water, but the fish was hanging off the side. I heard the snap of monofilament line, and the fish dropped back into the dark water and raced off, taking my heart with it, since it seemed certain that Mr. Lounsbury would never take me fishing again.

First Love

It was then that I learned that fishermen, at least the good ones, have more patience than anybody you could ever meet. He said it was no big deal, everybody did that, even experienced fishermen, so I shouldn't lose any sleep over it. "We'll get her next time. She'll be back, and so will we. She was a beauty, probably the biggest one I ever hooked up with here; might have been five pounds."

Redemption! What a beautiful thing! I was off the hook (pardon my fishing pun), and it sounded like fishing with him again would be an option. In the meantime, I vowed to come back to the dam as much as possible. Every night for the next week, as soon as supper was over, I'd grab my rod and gear and ride my bike down to the pond. I'd stay there until dark most nights, playing tag with the scores of bats that flew out of the old mill at night. They'd swoop down close to my head, so close I thought they'd knock my Red Sox cap off, but they never did. It was probably all a game to them, but I remember thinking what a pain in the butt it was.

I hadn't caught anything but a bunch of weeds every time I cast my rubber worm. I was discouraged, but realized with all of the casting being done that I was getting much more proficient at it. I was actually getting my worm close to where it was meant to go, so it wasn't all bad.

Saturday night came, and as had become my custom, I

headed down to the dam. Stowing my bike in the bushes, I went down the old path to the dam. As I broke through the overhanging brush into the clearing by the wall, I heard a monster splash.

Straight out in front of the wall there was a large circle of wavelets making their way toward me. Dropping my tackle bag, and releasing my hook from the eyelet on my rod, I let the rubber worm sail, and as it hit the water, a big swirl came out of the lily pads heading for my bait. I twitched and popped it, the way Mr. Lounsbury had taught me, and on the second twitch, my line went tight. Very tight!

Before I could even react, the water by the lily pads exploded. In the middle of the maelstrom was the prettiest thing I'd ever seen. It was a largemouth bass, and it was a big one. She just about tore the rod out of my hand when she hit the water again. My drag was already set, but the big bass kept ripping line off as I frantically reeled in every inch she gave back.

Like the bass that I'd lost for Mr. Lounsbury, this fish dug in as hard as she could, trying desperately to bury herself in the weeds that were everywhere in front of me. Remembering my lessons, I kept the line tight so that she wouldn't free herself. It was working; I was gaining ground on the fish, and getting it in closer to the wall.

I hadn't bought a net, yet; that would require having my father take me back to the sporting goods shop downtown. Still needing a few other things, I was trying to save some extra money. Now it was *Show Time* and no net!

Landing this fish wasn't going to be easy, so I worked it up into the grass near the base of the wall, reeling it in so close I could almost touch it. With a twenty pound leader on my worm, I decided to find out if it was strong enough to get this baby out of the water. Making sure I had my hook set good and tight, I reared back and pulled the fish right out of the water. The bass looked like one of the *Flying Wallendas* (the aquatic version, at least) as it went whizzing past my head and into the bushes behind me. I turned around, and there, in the middle of a bunch of scraggly brush and ragweed was my first-ever largemouth bass.

God, she was beautiful! The setting sun was sparkling off the green and black sides of the fish, and I made up my mind right there that getting that fish home as quickly as possible was the right thing to do. I tied it onto a stringer from my bag, and headed for my bike. It wasn't the easiest ride home, but the prize I had been dreaming about was in the saddle basket of my Schwinn, and I couldn't wait to show Mr. Lounsbury and my parents the *Greatest Fish on Earth*.

Of course, I went to Mr. Lounsbury's house first. Parking my bike, I jumped up on his porch and banged loudly on his door. He was reading the rest of the daily paper, but got up and came to the door. Standing there proudly, holding my fish, I waited for his excitement to match mine.

He was pretty shocked that I had caught a fish so large down at the dam. He probably thought it was the same one that I had helped get away the week before, but he never said anything like that. After staring at me and my bass, he congratulated me on the catch. He went to the back of his station wagon and opened his tackle box. He took out a scale, and hooked the fish onto it.

"Wow! Five and a half pounds! What a fish; I've never caught anything there bigger than four pounds, so this is quite the catch. But, Mark, I have to tell you something that may hurt your feelings. You should never have taken this fish out of the pond. She's a big breeder, and now her eggs won't be hatching anymore. I know you're pretty excited, and you should be, but this was the wrong thing to do."

Once again, it seemed, I had failed my mentor. My elation quickly turned to embarrassment, and I wanted to get out of there as quickly as I could. He could see all that in my face, so he assured me that it was just another *rookie* mistake. It was a lesson, he told me, one not to be forgotten. On that spring day in 1962, I learned about *catch and release,* a practice I follow most of the time to this day. If I keep a fish, and it's unusual that I do, it's because it's to be enjoyed as a meal, and not as a trophy.

Mr. Lounsbury and I continued to fish the dam after that. We both caught a lot of bass, releasing them all to catch another time. I never caught anything bigger than my first bass, but he landed a six and a half pounder there one night a couple years later. A largemouth that big in Massachusetts back then was a huge catch; I'd learn later on after moving to Florida that a fish that size wasn't even considered a trophy! Location, location, location!

The Beachhead

It was the summer of 1968. I had just graduated from high school, and had a job working downtown at a new sporting goods store. The shop was owned by a Taunton guy who was a well known gunsmith throughout the area. His name was Hank Duhamel, and the store was called Duhamel's Sporting Goods. Hank carried everything, but specialized in fishing and hunting gear.

He was, of course, the person to talk to about guns; any kind of gun. He had been shooting and repairing guns his whole life, and knew shotguns and hunting rifles better than anyone else in southeastern Massachusetts at the time. He was also an avid fisherman, but always deferred to his saltwater specialist, Bob Adams, when the subject turned to our favorite New England sport fish, the striped bass.

In those days, the best place in the country to catch stripers was along the East Coast, in the rivers and estuaries ranging from the Chesapeake Bay, north up into southern New England. Cape Cod and the islands of Martha's Vineyard and Nantucket were home to the big girls, the fifty-plus pounders that followed the huge bait schools up north in the spring and gorged themselves all summer long. By August, they were fattened up quite nicely, and were the target for every serious striper fisherman in the Northeast.

Bob was a police officer in Taunton, and worked part-time at the store. He had been fishing for big striped bass for years on the beaches of Cape Cod, and had dozens of catches to his credit. He had a *beach buggy* that he kept parked near the beach in Truro, out near the tip of the Cape. The camper sat in the lot at a local gas station, and was just one of many belonging to an elite group of anglers.

The dedicated, and sometimes crazy, members of this group were out there every weekend, or whenever the big bass were roaming the beaches. They would take their families or friends out to the beach, where they'd get out and let most of the air out of the tires. The campers were all 4-wheel drives, made for this kind of action. They'd drive up onto the sand and head down the beach to a colony of campers set up in a little community, where they'd park their vehicles and take their place amongst the group.

After listening to Bob tell stories about the monster stripers that his gang regularly caught off the beach, I guess I must have been a little starry-eyed when he told me about the 56-pounder he caught the weekend before. My mouth had hit the counter with his tale, and I could only dream what it would be like to land a fish that big. Then Bob popped the question.

"My wife's not going to the Cape this weekend; would you like to go with me? I'll show you how the wild men fish!"

"Seriously? I'll be packed in an hour!"

"No rush, it's only Tuesday. I usually leave around four on Friday afternoon. I'll check with Hank, and we'll open up the schedule for you. We've got enough weekend help; it won't be a problem. I already mentioned it to him this morning, and he didn't seem to mind."

"That's awesome! I'll work things out with my folks;

I'm sure they won't mind me going fishing with a cop. How much trouble could we get in, right?"

"If that's what you think, no problem. Let's get back to work; we've got some customers over in the fishing section."

Friday at four we loaded our gear up in the back of Bob's old Jeep Cherokee. The Jeep was pretty battered, but Bob explained to me that having an additional 4-wheel drive available to get off the beach was the best way to travel. Personally, I didn't care if we were going to ride camels onto the sands of Truro. I just wanted my chance to land a big striper!

Bob had an old Dodge Power Wagon, and that truck could probably drag a whale off the beach if you needed it to. The truck had a camper body attached, and he pulled a 16-foot aluminum boat behind it. He started the old truck up, and it roared to life. The throaty hum of that motor told me that it might look old, but that it was as good as advertised.

Bob had me take the wheel of the Jeep and follow him down the road for about a mile. We took a right at a dirt side road that led up into the dunes, and came to a stop where the road turned into sand. Bob jumped out of the camper, and I joined him. He instructed me to let most of the air out of the Jeep's tires, as he did the same to the Power Wagon.

"Time to get out there and find out if there's fish around to catch this weekend. Follow me to the campsite; it's not far, and most of the guys will already be there. I'll pull the camper in; park the Jeep right next to it on the left side."

He drove to the site, where he unhooked the boat trailer, and then parked the camper next to it. I pulled in next to him and got out. I started grabbing the gear, but Bob stopped me. "No need to move everything. We just leave it in the back, and get stuff when we need it. Nobody here's going to bother with anything. We're a fraternity out here; we all watch out for each other."

Bob took me around and introduced me to all of his friends. They were from all over Massachusetts, and one family had come up from New London, Connecticut. They had a huge bonfire going on the beach, and everybody settled in to talk about the fishing. The news wasn't great; there had been only two bass caught that day, and neither one of them was bigger than 10 pounds. It seemed that the huge schools of mackerel that had been everywhere for the past three weeks had disappeared. Apparently, the bass went with them.

Somebody shouted out that tomorrow was another day, and the mackerel might be back. With that, most of us headed off to get some sleep.

Four a.m. came pretty quickly. Bob got his camp stove going, and cooked up a batch of eggs and sausage. He brought some fresh rolls with him, too, so we chowed on the breakfast, wiping out most of it. Returning from the head, I saw that Bob had hooked up the boat to the Jeep and had it ready to go when I got back.

"Is there a launch ramp along here somewhere? I didn't see anything coming in, but figured there must be something."

Bob started laughing. "Yeah, I didn't tell you everything. Remember when I told you I was going to show you how the wild men fish? Well, you're about to find out real soon!"

He jumped in the truck and told me to stay there. He

drove down toward the water and stopped. He called me over. "We need to get the boat off the trailer, and then turn it around. Give me a hand rolling it off."

It was then that I realized what was coming next. All the gear was in the boat, ready to go. As we turned the bow towards the water, it all became crystal clear. We were launching into the oncoming waves!

To say I was a bit unnerved would be the biggest lie of 1968; I couldn't begin to fathom the concept of putting the bow of a 16-foot aluminum boat into what I guessed were two to three foot waves rolling into us. But I was there to fish, and if this was what was necessary to catch a big striper, then, dammit, let's go!

And go we did. As Bob edged the bow into the shallow water, he told me to get up in the front seat and hold on. He waited for a few minutes, saw the right wave coming towards us, and he pushed the boat into the swell. With dexterity I never saw coming, he jumped into the boat, started the motor and gunned it into the wave. The engine roared, and off we went.

Thinking back, things actually went pretty well. We were in deep water, heading away from the beach. Cool, I remember thinking; hell, that wasn't so bad.

The first thing we needed to do was catch some bait. The big bass here liked to feed on what was around, so filling the bait well was our priority. Bob had heard from one of the guys who had been casting plugs along the beach that he had seen a school of baitfish just off to the east. He turned the boat in that direction and told me to watch for activity up ahead.

We saw nothing. He went further east, and then turned

to deeper water to the south; still nothing. Bob pulled out some binoculars and began scanning the horizon. He saw a few other boats off to the west, so he turned towards them, our eyes burning the waters for any sign of bait. We were just cruising along hoping to get lucky; the weather was beautiful and it was great to be on the water, but our mission was to catch some big *pajama fish* (local slang for stripers). We tooled along, heading for the cluster of boats that was getting closer now.

"Holy shit! Bob, stop the boat! There's a whale right up in front of us; it's just laying there. It almost looks dead."

Bob cracked up. "Man, you are definitely a sorry-ass rookie! That's a sunfish. We see them out here all the time; they lay up on the surface and soak up the rays for hours. They're as crazy as the 'sun worshippers' on the beach."

The sunfish was about 7-8 feet across, and wasn't moving, or so it seemed. It looked like the *flounder from Hell* that you might see in your next nightmare. As Bob approached it, the fish moved off very slowly. It was apparently used to seeing the crazy fishermen out here in their tiny boats, and we didn't seem to bother it at all. Bob steered away from it once I had gotten a good look at it. It was a pretty strange sight, but at least we didn't have to worry about a *white whale* sending us to Davey Jones' locker.

We came up on the small fleet of boats that Bob had seen earlier. They were all bottom fishing for cod and haddock, but nobody was having much luck with those, either. They hadn't seen any sign of mackerel or the stripers we were stalking. Undaunted, Bob turned back to the east, towards our campsite, and cut the engine a few minutes later.

"Let's put some mackerel plugs on the trolling rods. I'll

run about a mile off the beach and see if we can pick up anything. I don't know what else to do other than this."

The trolling went on for several hours. We had eaten some sandwiches and drank some Cokes, but we seemed to be the only thing hungry that day. Around two o'clock we saw some birds diving off to the south, and we headed for them as soon as we could. The birds were working over a big school of bluefish that was chasing pogies. We grabbed the casting rods, already rigged with wire leaders for bluefish, and we started throwing plugs into the school.

We both hooked up immediately; our drags were screaming, and the blues were flying. We landed about ten fish, averaging 5-10 pounds, before they disappeared. Bob had thrown them in the box; one of the guys back at the beach had a smoker, and he'd be more than happy to smoke'em up to make us all some fish dip. That's about all we ever did with blues; they were too oily when they got bigger. We had some fun for about a half hour, though, so the day wasn't a total wash out. It was time to head in, announced the captain. I wasn't about to argue.

We were only about a half mile from the campsite, so it didn't take long to get there. The tide had changed, and the waves crashing on the beach were much bigger than when we launched that morning. I was about to ask Bob how he was going to handle this when he screamed over the motor noise "Hold on to your seat! We're going in and it's not going to be easy!"

His words rang in my ears. I looked towards the beach; it was coming up very fast. Bob increased the motor's speed and flew hell-bent towards it with a completely wild look on his face. I knew then that this was going to be what I really remembered about the day, because the launch this morning seemed like a cakewalk compared to what was coming.

We seemed to be going faster; Bob had the boat up on the crest of a wave, and we were actually surfing with a 16-foot aluminum boat! It was scaring the hell out of me, but I didn't have a lot of time to do much more than hold on for dear life; the beachhead was in my face. The wave started its break and thrust the tiny boat at the beach like a leaf on the wind; and then we hit.

I remember thinking that every tooth in my head seemed to explode, and my entire body screamed at me. I realized that we had stopped, very abruptly, but we were now sitting up on the high-water mark, and we were both still alive. I couldn't believe it! Bob told me later that I was screaming my ass off, and I still don't remember if that's true or not; it's not that far-fetched to be looked upon as a fabrication. I probably was!

There was a crowd of our fellow campers standing together on the beach, and as I somehow managed to crawl out of the boat, a cheer went up from all of them. I was a rookie, and I had just made my first *crash landing*, a feat that had them all yelling and clapping. My initiation complete, I was being welcomed into the ranks of the wild-eyed, crazy anglers of Truro, Massachusetts.

Trout Fishing

Mr. Lounsbury had taken me fishing many times over the years after we first became friends in that summer of 1962. He had introduced me to trout fishing in the local streams in the spring of 1963. The Segregansett River flowed in, out and all about the town of Dighton, where we lived. It was a slow, meandering brook at its headwaters, but it turned into a brackish estuary as it poured into the Taunton River in the south end of town.

The Commonwealth of Massachusetts had a spring stocking of nursery-raised trout throughout the state, and the Segregansett, or the *"Seggy"* as we locals referred to it, got its fair share. On Opening Day, everyone with a rod and reel would be at the pools nearest the rural roads of our town hoping to catch one of the bigger fish that had been stocked.

Occasionally someone would actually catch one bigger than the norm, but a just barely legal fish was the usual catch. It didn't stop me from being at the stream at daybreak on Saturday and Sunday, because catching fish was what it was all about, and it was fun!

I had built myself a little ultralight rod, using the tip section of my Dad's old rod and a display base from the sporting goods store. I bought a new-to-the-market Shakespeare ultralight reel, filled it with 4-pound test and mounted it on my homemade rod. That became my *weapon of choice* for chasing down the brookies and rainbows that called the Seggy their home, and I had a blast catching every one of them.

Tiring of the stocked pools by the roadside, I decided to explore the river a little more closely. I started going deeper into the woods, away from the crowd, and into areas that weren't fished much. I discovered hidden pools with hold-over trout from years past that had swum out of the stocked areas and into the woods.

With my trusty little ultralight rod and reel in hand, I would march off into the snarls of briars and vines that seemed to grow everywhere along the banks of the stream. After years of not being used, the pathways had been over-whelmed by the invasive growth, so it had become very difficult to navigate your way through the maze. I would literally get on my belly sometimes to crawl through to the next clearing.

My efforts were rewarded with the discovery of several nice fishing holes; one in particular was about four feet deep and thirty feet long before it turned back into a shallow stream. The pool was surrounded by brush and vines except in a couple of spots. To fish here, I had to get on my knees or my belly, once again, to be able to pitch a night crawler downstream into the deeper water.

The results were worth the effort! I caught so many nice trout here that it became my primary target when fishing the Seggy. It was my *go-to* spot; I once caught a rainbow trout, definitely a holdover from a few years prior that was almost three pounds. The colors of that fish are still vivid in my memory.

After crawling and scraping my way through the brush

for about a year to get to this spot, I was at work one day telling a friend about my secret spot. My conversation was overheard by one of the managers in my department, and he asked me if my spot had a rock cliff behind it about twenty-five feet high. It did.

He laughed and told me that pool was on his land. He and his family had purchased an old farmhouse on the main road that went back to the 1700's. It was more of a *Gentleman's farm* for him, since he had a full-time job, but the family did have a horse and grew some corn on the property. He told me that I could park in the back of his barn and follow the old dirt path down to the stream, where I would end up almost being on top of my fishing hole.

I took him up on his offer many times; the walk down to the pool was about a quarter mile, much shorter, and certainly much easier, than my original walk of close to a mile through briar-covered brush. I continued to catch some nice trout in there, but I started yearning for the big ones that my old mentor was catching, and my trips into the woods ended.

Which segues back to Mr. Lounsbury; Fred, as I was now allowed to call him, had been fishing the big ponds of Cape Cod for years, and would come home with *Polaroids* of some incredible rainbows and brook trout. But the most awesome photo he ever showed me was one of a six and a half-pound brown trout, something I had never even seen, let alone caught. He had sunk the hook again!

Fred took me to Cape Cod with him a few times to chase trout. His favorite spot was Cliff Pond, in Nickerson State Park, in Brewster. The park also boasted two other ponds, Little Cliff and Flax, and all three were stocked heavily by the state. But Cliff was the biggest and deepest, and according to Fred, this was where the big browns were. We always fished there.

Fred had a system to catch trout that I had never used before. He would tie a long leader to a small swivel, and place a sliding half ounce sinker to the line above the swivel. This allowed for a long cast, and a free-running line if a fish took off with the bait. He used night crawlers for bait, wrapped on a small hook. After casting out to the deeper water, he'd put the rod in a rod holder set into the sand; he'd then attach an offset small bobber to the line between the second and third eyes of the rod, dropping the bobber down to the water below his rod. The bail was left open so if a trout took the bait, the line would move out cleanly through the bobber and let the fish take off. The bobber would rise up out of the water on a hit, so it served as a visual enhancement. It was pretty cool!

I learned how to use this method to catch a lot of trout whenever I got to go with Fred. I never did catch a big *brownie*, but I was fortunate enough to catch my fair share of nice-sized brookies and browns over the years. My greatest success was with rainbows, though, consistently catching better than average fish, generally running in the 3-4 pound range.

The Sailfish

In the early summer of 1969, I introduced my friend, Bruce Perry, to trout fishing in the deep ponds of Cape Cod. Bruce and I had become close friends, attending Southeastern Massachusetts University (now the University of Massachusetts – Dartmouth), and commuting to school several days a week together. Of course, fishing adventures had eventually come up on a regular basis.

Bruce became interested in learning more, so we made a plan to drive to Nickerson State Park to fish Cliff Pond. I gave Bruce a list of tackle he needed, like Fred had done for me years earlier, and we both looked forward to spending the upcoming weekend fishing for trout.

We had decided to drive to the park on Friday afternoon and do some fishing that night. We'd stay overnight that night and Saturday, too, sleeping on the beach in sleeping bags. We brought a camp stove and provisions along, with the hope of some pan-fried trout as the main course throughout the weekend. We were all set to go.

Bruce called me on Thursday morning with a new plan. "I've got a Sailfish in the garage. I was thinking we should take that with us to fish from."

"What the hell is a Sailfish?"

"It's a little sailboat. It's only fourteen feet long, and it's not very heavy. We could sail it out into the middle of the pond and fish from it. It should be pretty cool. What do you think?"

I had never been on a sailboat of any size, so I really didn't know what to think. But the thought of being able to fish the deeper water in the middle of the day caught my interest. "What the hell? Why not? Can we fit it on the car?"

The car in question was my '65 Mustang Fastback, my pride and joy. We wouldn't be able to put it in the car, so we'd have to attach some roof racks to carry it to the Cape.

"No problem. My Dad's got some racks with suction cups. We can use those; we'll just have to make sure we tie it down good."

It was decided; the sailfish would be part of our expedition. On Friday, I went to Bruce's house. He was waiting for me; he was holding the roof racks, and the Sailfish was on the grass next to the driveway. My first impression of the little sailboat wasn't good. It had a white hull, but the deck was a bright red, and the sail, furled up next to the boat, looked like it had a red stripe running through it.

"Damn! We're gonna look like the *'Hahvid Sailing Team'* in that thing! I didn't bring my blue blazer with me; should I go get it?"

Bruce just laughed. "Come on, man, I had a lot of fun sailing this boat over the years. Give me a break, and let's just see if we can't catch some fish from it."

"Okay, okay! I won't make fun of your silly little boat again. Let's get it loaded and get on the road."

We followed the normal route to the Cape. The traffic had been picking up as we got closer, and by the time we got across the Sagamore Bridge and onto the Cape we had lost a lot of time. It took us another two hours to get to the park in Brewster. We paid the entrance fee and drove into the park, following the signs for Cliff Pond. It didn't take long before we found a nice parking spot near the water.

The car hadn't cooled down before I was walking the beach, casting a silver MirrOlure. Fred had told me that he had been having a lot of fun picking up fish at dawn and at dusk with both the silver and the gold edition of this lure, so we had both brought a few of each.

Bruce joined me on the beach and started casting the gold model. We figured we'd find out in a hurry which one was working, but within seconds of each other we both hooked up. Our reward was a pair of pretty rainbows about 18" long. They were almost identical. "They must have just unloaded these babies from the nursery. They look like twins," I said, releasing my first one. We had stopped for dinner before we got to the park, so fresh trout wasn't on the menu for that night.

We continued casting the MirrOlures for about an hour, and we both kept catching trout. The majority of the fish were rainbows, roughly the same size as our first two, but we also picked up some nice brookies that were 14-16 inches. The action slowed right around dark, so we called it a night. The four-hour drive had wiped us out, so we decided to concentrate on an early day of fishing Saturday.

I woke up first around five. The sun hadn't broken the horizon yet, but I was awake and ready to go. I lit my lantern and walked up the beach, away from Bruce. I had everything I needed to get started on some bottom fishing, using Fred's trusted system. Loading my hook up with a fat night crawler, I threw it out as far as it would go. I set it in a rod holder and affixed the bobber onto the free line. I found a rock to sit on and made myself comfortable, certain that a nice trout would come along some time soon.

After a few minutes I heard Bruce walking up the beach towards me. I gave him the usual razzing about *sleeping in* and he took it all in stride. We chatted a bit, and then he decided to go get his gear and join me in the pursuit. While we were busy talking, I hadn't noticed my bobber coming out of the water.

As he walked away the bobber fell back into the water. Certain that my quarry had dropped the worm and headed off, I was surprised to see line peeling off the spool. Excited, I grabbed my rod out of the holder and waited for the trout to take the bait. The fish slowed up and I set the hook; the battle was underway!

Bruce hadn't heard a thing until the trout jumped out of the water. On hearing the loud splash of a big fish he had turned around to watch. It had gotten light enough to see the fish at a distance, but still too dark to distinguish what species it was. My instincts told me it was a rainbow from the way it raced to the surface so quickly, but I secretly hoped that the fish on the end of my line was the elusive big brownie that had previously avoided me.

That fish ran hard from left to right, down deep, then it would fly out of the water like it was shot from a cannon. I had six-pound test monofilament on my brand new Mitchell 400 reel, and the drag was screaming! I hung on and worked it in towards the beach. When it was about forty feet in front of us, the trout made one last jump; the sun was lighting up the sky a bit by that time, reflecting off the beautiful colors of a big rainbow.

Bruce was stunned! He watched as it came closer; I waded out a little bit with my net, and scooped the fish up.

"Holy shit!" he yelled. "I can't believe the size of that trout!" Like me, he had only seen the small stocked trout in the Segregansett River back home before coming here, and he was impressed.

"She's a beauty, that's for sure! Grab the scale out of my box, will ya?"

Bruce grabbed the scale and gently hooked my prize onto it. It was four and a half pounds, the biggest trout I had ever caught. Quickly deciding that this fish was not going on the menu, I gently put it back into the water. Having learned my lesson years before with my big bass, releasing her was the obvious decision for me. She seemed happy to have another chance at living, and I think she winked as she swam away.

Bruce baited up his rod, and we both cast out our night crawlers; Bruce to the left and me to the right. After setting the rods up on their holders and placing our bobbers, we sat back down on the rock. We talked about a bunch of things, never taking our eyes off our bobbers. The anticipation of another big trout had us both pretty amped up.

Unfortunately, we didn't get a chance at another lunker. Nothing was biting, so we decided to go back to pitching the MirrOlures from the beach. We started catching rainbows and brookies just like the night before, so we selected a half dozen to cook up for breakfast a little later. I even caught a brownie about twenty inches, but it wasn't the giant I was looking for, so it, too, was released.

There's nothing like pan-fried fish, but fresh trout is the best, in my opinion. Its delicate flavor goes well with anything, so it was a nice fit with some scrambled eggs Bruce cooked up for us. A slight breeze had come up, but we weren't smart enough to get someplace sheltered, so we had a bit of sand mixed in with our trout and eggs. It wasn't the first time for that; eating outside on a beach sort of invites the sand to join you, but it still tasted great!

We took a break for a couple of hours after breakfast. We threw some bathing suits on at the nearby swimming beach, and spent some time relaxing. Bruce was anxious to get his Sailfish in the water, so we headed back to our campsite. The sun was directly overhead, and I remember thinking it wasn't the best time to go fishing, but the boat was going to get us out over the deeper water, so maybe it was worth a shot.

We took the ties off the Sailfish and lifted it off the Mustang, bringing it out to the water's edge, and went back to get some gear. Since the boat didn't have a lot of room, I suggested we each just take a rod with a few MirrOlures. We could jig them off the bottom to see if we could get a strike; hopefully they'd attract some of those bigger fish that were supposedly down there.

With everything onboard, we pushed the Sailfish out into the water. Bruce manned the tiller and the sail from the stern, and I sat up front, eager to see if this idea actually worked. He got the sail up and we started to catch a little wind. The boat moved away from the beach, heading for the *promised land;* we were about to go where the big fish lived!

It didn't take long for Bruce to get us on our way. We were talking about something going on back home when a big breeze from the opposite direction hit the sail. Bruce hadn't seen it coming and had no time to correct things, so the sail came flying at me like a train coming down the tracks. "Of course I ducked! Wouldn't you?"

By jumping to avoid getting hit in the head by the sail, I upset the weight distribution of the boat. As I dove out of the way, and the sail did its job, the whole boat lifted out of the water and we both went ass-over-teakettle into the pond. My earlier suggestion to keep our bathing suits on had turned out to be prophetic, but that wasn't the big deal.

We both lost our rods in the flip. They were at the bottom of Cliff Pond, about a hundred feet below us, and we were trying to get the damned Sailfish upright so we could go back in. I had put my lures in a small plastic box, and stuck it into my pocket, so they were safe; Bruce had lost everything. It wasn't good!

We struggled with the Sailfish until Bruce managed to get the sail closed up. Once he did that, we were able to swim back to shore, pushing the Sailfish in front of us. When we hit the beach I said "Let's get this friggin' boat on top of the car and head home! That's enough excitement for this weekend."

Bruce didn't argue with me; he knew that losing my brand new rig had really pissed me off, and he had lost his, too. So we loaded up the boat and anything else we had out and left the park. It turned out to be the last time I ever fished in that pond. I had lost interest in fishing for a few years after our weekend debacle, due to some life moments (getting married, having a baby and working at least two jobs all the time), but I ended up turning my attention to saltwater angling when I did go back to the water.

Back to the Future

Sometime during that same summer, and I'm not sure chronologically if this was before the Sailfish story (I think it may have been), Bruce Perry and I had driven down to Cape Cod and signed on to go out on a charter boat for a day-long trip. The party boat was a typical bottom-dunking excursion, with about fifty people on board. The target was cod, haddock and pollock; they were the best and most common of the cold water species in Cape Cod Bay.

Once the Captain had the big boat underway, one of the mates came around and asked us if we'd like to join the *pool* for the day. It was five dollars each, and the pot was given to the angler with the biggest (weight) fish, regardless of species. We both threw our money into the big jar he had, and didn't think much more about it.

Until later, of course. The fishing was terrible; we weren't catching anything of value. Sea robins (an extremely ugly bottom scavenger) were the only fish that seemed to want our bait, so the Captain decided to try to locate a mackerel school. There are huge schools of Boston mackerel that invade New England waters each summer, and the excitement generated getting into a school of them had saved many a captain's butt.

Boston, or tinker, mackerel are not large fish. Fifteen to twenty inches back then was about average. What they lacked in size they made up for in toughness. Like every mackerel species in our oceans, these fish didn't give up; they were tenacious and a lot of fun when you got into a big school. My father used to love to eat them when they were fresh; he'd gut them and fry them up whole, then pick the meat off the bones. I have to admit I enjoyed quite a few over the years, as well.

Our Captain called every boat in a twenty-mile radius to find someone who had located a mackerel school, but, like everything else that day, the macks weren't around. After about two hours he finally threw in the towel and announced we'd be going back to bottom fishing as soon as he got over a rock bed he was heading for.

When he slowed the boat down and started a slow circling pattern the mates started throwing buckets of chum overboard. I never saw anyone chum the way they were doing it on this rock pile that day. They must have laid out three times as much in this spot as they had on our morning location. We all dropped our lines down, and started the wait.

People around us started getting some hits. Mixed in with more sea robins were a couple of pollock and a small fluke. Bruce had pulled in a sea robin, but I hadn't gotten a nibble. But finally my rod tip took a quick bounce on the rail, and I picked it up, waiting for my opportunity. Tightening the slack up a bit, I felt a pretty good tug, so I pulled back and hooked into something.

The rental rod wasn't heavy-duty, so it drew some attention from the others on the stern rail when they saw a good bend in my rod. Most of them moved aside to give me some room, and a few minutes later I brought in the first codfish of the day. A cheer went up, because that's what everybody wanted on the end of their line, and they were all hoping that we were on top of a bunch more. The mate weighed it; it was seven-pounds, two ounces, the heaviest fish of the day!

We fished for over an hour after that, but nothing crossed the rail bigger than my now beautiful seven-pounder. The only competition in the closing minutes was another cod, about three pounds, and a pollock a little smaller.

The Captain came over the intercom telling everybody to bring up their lines and give their rods to the mates. It was over! I had the top fish! Once we were heading back in, the mate came over and handed me a wad of bills. I gave him ten bucks and thanked him for his help.

Sitting down to count my winnings, I was shocked. I counted it, and counted it again, but the number was the same. I had just won $210 for my prize catch. It's the most money per pound I've ever gotten for a fish, and I got to bring it home, cook it up and enjoy it. It was a very tasty meal!

Author's Note: I called this chapter "Back to the Future" because today a seven-pound cod is considered a good catch. Back then, people were getting twenty to forty pounders on most of the charters. Like everywhere else, fishing on Cape Cod has changed a lot in the last forty years!

Fifty Pounds or Bust!

Every man, woman or child who's ever wet a line in search of a striped bass had a goal in mind, at least in my day. If you were a serious angler, you wanted to join the list of people before you that had successfully landed a fifty-pound striper. I don't know of a single guy I ever fished with who didn't want to land a monster over fifty.

It didn't matter if you were surfcasting from the beaches and jetties of New England, live-lining off of Cape Cod or working the birds on a tidal flat on an outgoing tide; that was the goal. The big one! The Big Mama of Pajama Fish! Everybody wants one; so few get them.

This story is about a good friend of mine who passed away years ago of cancer. His name was Dave Mello, but we called him Rocky. He became one of my closest striper buddies, and we spent a tremendous amount of time chasing the stripers and bluefish of Cape Cod together.

Along with Bruce Whowell, another striper-crazed fanatic, we shared a great kinship for about eight years before my life, and his death, put an end to our band of brothers. I still think about those days and the character that was Rocky Mello; he was a great fishing companion who never ran out of stories, and he always kept us laughing.

Rocky was the kind of guy who would love to be reincarnated as a striped bass. I can picture him teaching the other bass how not to get caught. "No, don't chase that thing; it's a piece of surgical tubing, you flounder!" or maybe "Check the rocks first to see if there's any big humans standing on them before you start hitting everything in sight!" To catch fish, you need to become the fish, so my vision of Rocky reversing the process is something I've always chuckled about.

But on to his story; Rocky's father was an avid fisherman, who raised two sons. Like his father, Rocky loved to fish. It didn't matter where, or for what, but his preference was striper fishing. His dad was a lifetime striper guy who taught him everything he knew about catching them.

His dad's favorite place was at the Railroad Bridge in Buzzard's Bay on Cape Cod in Massachusetts. He fished on the far side of the Cape Cod Canal, driving over the Bourne Bridge and then working his way back down to the Railroad Bridge.

He was an old-timer and used a big heavy bait-casting rod and reel most of the time. He would use eel skin rigs, which consisted of attaching an eel skin over a large hook, which attached to another line that was heavily weighted. After casting it out, the weight would take it to the bottom, where the skin would fill with water and wiggle just like a live eel. The trick was to get it in close to the bridge pilings, where eels naturally occurred, and where big bass came to eat them.

He taught Rocky how to fish like this, and together they spent lots of time chasing down the big girls that frequented the bridge. Neither Rocky nor his dad had ever caught a bass over fifty pounds, but they had both been very successful over the years, landing many fish in the thirty to forty-pound range.

Rocky's older brother hadn't fished since he was a kid. Unlike his younger sibling, he never really cared for it much. Despite his father's urgings, he continued to show no interest in fishing for years. But one time, at a family event, Rocky and his father goaded the brother into joining them for a night of striper fishing at the Railroad Bridge. I can't swear to it, but I'm guessing there was liquor involved.

The three of them loaded up their gear and headed for their father's favorite spot. When they got there, Rocky baited up and cast his rod out into the swirls at the base of the bridge. His father was tied up for a while getting his and his other son's rod ready, but after a short time all three rods were in the water. The men sat down to enjoy the evening and wait for a hit.

A couple of hours had gone by with no results, but the tide turned around and got the water moving again. Just before one o'clock, his brother's rod started bending and line screamed out. He knew enough to get up and pull back, which he did; the hook was set, and he had a fish that was fighting like hell on the end of his line.

The fish did everything it could to get itself free around the pilings, but Joe was able to keep him away enough. The fish moved off to the right, and then back to the left. This dance continued for four hours, until Joe was able to finally wear the big fish out. Rocky and his dad climbed down onto the rocks and managed to grab it, pulling it out of the water.

The striped bass was huge! They dragged it up onto the road that runs along the Canal and saw just how big it was. Rocky's father went and got his tackle box scale and hooked it onto the fish's jaw. Lifting it, they all watched as the needle went to fifty-three pounds!

Of course, Rocky and his dad were ecstatic! The fifty-pound striper that they longed to catch was lying on the road in front of them, caught by the son who never wanted to fish. As the two of them danced around and hugged Joe, congratulating him for his catch, he looked at the both of them and said…

"You guys are nuts! You call this fun? I just worked my ass off for four hours and my body feels sore just about everywhere. I can tell you right now, don't ever try to get me out fishing again!"

Dave "Rocky" Mello died in his forties never having joined the club. I hope he's in Striper Heaven having a hell of a good time. I hear every fish there is over fifty!

Hello, Cape Cod Canal!

In 1975 my wife became pregnant with our second child. Since I was out of town working when my son was born a few years earlier, I promised her (and myself) that I would be there with her this time. In order for me to assist in our child's birth, we signed up for a Lamaze birthing class at the local hospital.

There were quite a few couples there, but after a little while I noticed a woman on the other side of the room who I knew from our high school days. At the end of the class, we went over to my acquaintance and said hello. Her husband got our interest when he invited us to join them for a hot fudge sundae at Friendly's.

My wife and I were dyed-in-the-wool *Chocoholics* who wasted no time in responding affirmatively. We not only joined them that night, but did so after every class for weeks. At one of our ice cream parties, Bruce asked me if I ever fished before.

That was the beginning of a long friendship. Bruce asked me if I'd like to join him and another guy for some striper fishing, and I jumped at the chance. Two nights later, I met Rocky Mello and the three of us headed off to the Cape Cod Canal in search of the big ones.

Little did I know at the time that the hours we spent on that first night would turn into hundreds, maybe thousands, of hours over the next few years. Our wives began to realize that our fishing trips could mean they might not see us until sometime the next day, which might have made all of them happy, who knows?

The Cape Cod Canal was built and is maintained by the Army Corps of Engineers. They built roads on both sides that travel the entire length of the Canal, but these roads aren't open to the public. So to access the Canal, you had to find places to park, and then walk down to the access road. Once on the road, we would go to specific spots where we had previously been successful.

Alongside the roads were streetlights, and each of the poles were numbered. Rocky had been keeping a log of light numbers for years, so we would usually follow his lead and go to the light he named. There were lights on one side that were great for bass on an incoming, but useless on an outgoing. There were lights that were excellent for bluefish, but never gave up any bass. A great light on one side of the Canal didn't mean the light opposite you would have any fish. And so on; you get the picture.

With Rocky's guidance we became very adept at catching fish. Our tales led to other guys joining us once in a while, but the core group stayed the steadiest. We fished every Wednesday night throughout striper season, and either Friday or Saturday night. If we went on a Friday night and did well, we usually headed back on Saturday night, too.

Our excursions became all-night affairs on the weekend. We'd head down after dinner and fish well past sunrise the next morning. We'd travel from one end of the Canal to the other, crossing over if we weren't doing well. We always seemed to find at least one or two lonely fish; it's what kept us going back. I'm sure you know the feeling if you're a die-hard angler.

You Dirty Rat!

The Canal is lined on both sides with large rocks, like a typical jetty at most inlets around the country. Any of you who fish at night on the water know that it can get pretty cold, even in the middle of summer, when you're sitting on one of those rocks waiting for the fish to show up. So, in order to battle the chill, we used to stop at a liquor store and pick up a pint of blackberry brandy on those cooler nights.

Anyone who drinks alcohol knows, at least deep down, that it really doesn't warm you up, but it can get your brain a little toasty on a cold damp night. Believe me, I'm not trying to encourage anybody to drink; I hardly drink anything at all anymore after doing some very stupid things while inebriated. But on this one particular night, we made our obligatory stop and purchased a pint of brandy.

We got to one of our favorite lights and started fishing. The three of us were casting lures for over an hour with no results, so Bruce suggested we cross over to the east side and spend some time there. We hadn't fished that area much, so we decided to split up and work different lights until we got something. I went off by myself to the north, while Bruce and Rocky headed in the opposite direction.

I had kept walking further away for a couple of hours, but only had a quick hit with no hook set. The tide had slowed down to almost slack, so I decided it would be a good time to take a nap. Standing my rod up in the rocks and putting my gear down next to me, I pulled out my brandy and took a couple hits, figuring it might help me sleep.

I used to wear L.L. Bean wool CPO shirts all the time. They were normally warm enough to keep the dampness out at night, and easy to shed if it warmed up in the morning. They offered another advantage; the two big pockets were great for carrying tackle or a snack.

I found myself a couple of rocks that were smooth enough to get comfortable and settled in, falling asleep pretty quickly. Not sure how long I had been dozing, but I was awakened by something that didn't feel right. Opening my eyes, I realized that *something* was a large rat! It was on my stomach, trying to get the sandwich in my pocket.

I jumped up fast, and with a single swipe sent that damned thing skittering across the rocks. After landing and getting his balance, the ugly creature just stared back at me before heading back down into the rocks. I went for the blackberry brandy with a vengeance.

It was my first encounter with a rat up close and personal, and it had scared the hell out of me! Visions of him eating my face danced through my stream of consciousness. With my hands still shaking a bit, I tore into the brandy, and emptied the entire pint in a blink.

That qualified as one of those stupid things I was talking about earlier. The brandy got into my blood in a hurry. With an empty stomach and a cold sweat, the liquor took over what I had left of my faculties.

Needing to get away from the rat, I grabbed my gear and took off, moving further to the north. It was probably a mile away when I decided to sit and try to get myself calmed down. I started throwing my lure out into the water in front of me, retrieving it slowly as I always did. On one of my retrieves, the hook got caught on the bottom.

My life seemed to be in slow motion. I tugged and tugged, and my line kept going out. I'd reel in, my line would go out. I heard a noise behind me; it was Bruce and Rocky. Bruce yelled out to me.

"Hey, you got something pretty big! How long have you had it hooked?"

In my drunken stupor, I answered back that I was caught on the bottom and couldn't get my lure loose. The two of them just about cracked their ribs laughing at me. When he finally caught his breath, Bruce told me that my drag was screaming and that I wasn't caught on the bottom.

"I'll bet you fifty bucks that you could never get that lure stuck on the bottom in this current. It only weighs a half ounce. You've got a big bass on the end of your line, man! Bring it in!"

Armed with this knowledge, but still stupidly drunk, I then made the decision to try to land the bass. The reason my line kept going out was because my drag was too loose for the fish I had on, so I tightened down on the drag a bit. It turned out to be a bit too much; the fish dug in and I was rewarded with that feeling we all get when we lose a nice fish. It was gone!

My friends got the biggest kick out of that. They had watched the whole show, and they busted my ass about that one that got away for a long time. Even after I told them the rat story, they had no sympathy and showed no mercy. But that's what your fishing buddies do, right?

The Red Coach Grill

On the northern end of the Canal (which is actually known as the East End) there's a state park called Scusset Beach. As the name implies, it was a daytime attraction for beachgoers and sun worshippers, but at night it was known more as a fishing destination. The Canal emptied into Cape Cod Bay, which led into Massachusetts Bay and the cities of Plymouth (yes, the one with the rock) and Boston.

The East End wasn't one of our normal haunts; it was the furthest point from our homes and we had historically always done well closer to the West End. But one night, after several hours of walking and casting with no fish on deck we decided to take a ride up to Scusset Beach. It was another one of those cool, damp nights in late September and the fog had set in on the Canal.

Depending on the weather, September could either be a bust or a bonus. If the weather cooled down quickly, the huge bait pods would start to move south, which got the stripers and blues moving with them. If things stayed fairly warm, it had the opposite effect. This September was one of the latter, and we were still picking up a lot of good fish.

The reason we went up to Scusset was mostly because our catch numbers had been dropping significantly in our last couple of trips. The bass were starting to move out, going south into Rhode Island waters and Long Island Sound, but we were hearing reports that big bass were still hitting around the Cape, so we kept at it. Our fishing season was short, so stretching it out even a week or two was our goal every year, and this year was no different.

Rocky had told us that sometimes the stragglers from northern New England waters would hang out in Cape Cod Bay a little later, so that was enough to get my truck moving in that direction. We hoped it was worth the effort.

Back in those days we used to make our own surgical tubing lures. We bought the tubing, spray painted it white, and then cut it into the appropriate sizes. For bass we used smaller-sized tubing, but for blues we went to a larger size. We used bullet head sinkers that free-lined on a long wire leader, and worked the tubing onto a long-shanked hook. The finished product looked like a white eel, which proved to be a killer lure for us.

When we got to the East End, the tide was ripping hard into the bay. I can't tell you why, but I decided to throw on a bluefish tube, while Bruce and Rocky stayed with the smaller bass edition. They set up right in front of where we parked and started casting. I walked up the road about a hundred yards and started pitching my lure into some fast-moving water. There were big swirls and eddies being created by the outgoing tide just off the rocks about fifty yards out.

On my second cast I had a jarring hit; my drag started screaming loud enough for my buddies to hear. They started working their way up to me, casting as they walked until they reached my location. I told them to switch over to a big tube; I was pretty certain that my fish was a blue. It was fighting like it was snagged in the butt, and I was struggling to get it turned.

By the time I landed mine, both of them were hooked

up with one of its traveling companions. My catch turned out to be a sixteen-pounder. Figuring that we had hit the *Mother lode,* I ran back to my truck and grabbed a box of heavy duty trash bags. We used to transport all of our fish like that; it kept our trucks smelling a little better that way!

By the time I got back to the rocks my friends had landed both of their fish. I threw the bags down on the rocks and grabbed my rod. On the first cast, I got a hit, but didn't hook it. Throwing it out again, I was rewarded with another smash attack on my lure, as were both of my buddies as soon as they hit the water.

We were sitting on a very hungry school of big bluefish. These fish had been bulking up on the huge bait schools all summer long, and they were all fat and sassy. The average weight of our fish at the end of the night was probably around fifteen pounds each; they were heavy and full of piss and vinegar.

We continued to hook up on almost every cast for about an hour. The fish were wearing us down, since we weren't only fighting them, but also an extremely fast tide. We were talking about calling it quits and heading home when I got hit so hard I almost lost my balance on the rocks.

This monster took off like a speeding bullet; I was sure it could also leap tall buildings in a single bound if it wanted to. The fish dove deeper into the rip, and I started thinking that this girl might not join her friends in the bags. It was tearing line off my spool at an alarming rate, and I was having a hard time keeping up with it. I tightened down on my drag just enough to start turning her.

I finally wore her down. The fish started to give in to the pressure I was putting on it, and I got it turned, heading for home. With a last minute splash and a burst of energy, it got a little dicey getting her in, but with help from Rocky we managed to pull it out of the water and up onto the rocks.

She tipped the scales at twenty-one pounds. It was by far the biggest bluefish I had ever caught; I had never even seen one that big in all my years fishing. I remember telling my friends that at times I felt like I had a refrigerator on the end of my line; its power was that overwhelming.

Pound for pound, the bluefish is one of the strongest and toughest fish in the water. Our tackle wasn't very heavy; I used seventeen-pound mono back then, on a medium-light seven-foot rod. The equipment had served me well; I had landed several stripers in the thirty-pound class and never felt overmatched.

My biggest striped bass was forty-two pounds. At half the weight, this bluefish had almost stripped and smoked my reel. It was a blast! I live in Florida now, and I've heard stories of guys picking up bluefish off the beaches here. But the Florida blues are generally small, running just a few pounds apiece. I've not fished for them here, but I imagine they would be a lot of fun on ultralight tackle in the surf.

Back to the Canal; Bruce, Rocky and I landed twenty-two blues in two hours that night. We probably had about three hundred pounds bagged up when we called it a night. My fish won top honors, but every fish was big, as I mentioned earlier. The smallest was twelve pounds, but there were only a couple like that; most were in the fifteen to sixteen range. It was some of the most intense fishing I've ever done.

So why am I calling this chapter "The Red Coach Grill?" The Red Coach was a nice restaurant about halfway between our normal fishing grounds and our homes. The Head Chef there was an amiable man who loved fresh fish. He had a special striped bass plate that was his signature dish, so he was always ready to buy fresh bass from us. He'd pay us two dollars a pound for a whole fish; he didn't really want bluefish, but he agreed to take whatever we had for the ridiculous price of twenty-five cents per pound. The only rule was that we had to be there by midnight, or he'd be gone.

We sold him a lot of fish over the years, using the cash for gas and expenses. Having several bags of bluefish to sell, our plan all along was to stop at the restaurant and make a deal with Alan, the chef. But there was a bit of a snag in that plan; we were miles from where we usually fished and the clock was ticking.

The blitz was steady for two hours before we stopped at eleven. It took us a while to get our gear and the fish back to my van, so by the time we got on the road it was close to 11:30. Knowing it would be almost impossible to get to the restaurant by midnight, I put the pedal to the metal a little bit more than usual. I was fortunately not tagged for speeding, but we were twenty miles away from our usual departure point, which put the pressure on me big-time!

We had a plan to just get whatever we could for all the fish from Alan, and throw them in his walk-in refrigerator. It was quarter past twelve as I pulled off the highway and made the turn into the Red Coach, and the first thing we noticed was that there was no sign of life at all. We went around the back, praying that Alan's car would be there, but it wasn't. He was gone and we had a van full of fish.

You know how you're always supposed to have a Plan

B? We didn't. I drove toward home and when we were about fifteen minutes away, Bruce came up with an idea.

There was another guy who fished with us on occasion. He didn't have quite the dedication to it as we did, but he was a good guy, and we enjoyed his company. Mike had a smoker, and had always told us if we wanted him to smoke something for us we should just stop by his house and leave it.

We got to Mike's just before one. Of course, he and his family were all sleeping, but his dog's barking put an end to that. He looked out the window and saw the three of us standing in his driveway. A minute later he came out and wanted to know what was going on.

We told him we had some bluefish, and that we had missed the chef at the Red Coach. We needed his help; would he put our fish in his extra refrigerator and smoke some of it for us when he had some time. We were quite generous, and told him he could keep as much as he wanted to; give it to all his friends and family if he wanted to.

As I said, Mike was a good guy. He agreed to take the blues and smoke them up, but when he saw all the bags of fish in the back of my van, he damned near had a heart attack!

I think he might have buried most of them in his back yard. It probably would have taken him two weeks to smoke three hundred pounds of oily fish, so I'm sure he didn't get to most of them. I never asked him for any; it was too embarrassing! His wife never let him fish with us again, and we were all *persona non grata* at his place, but like I said (twice, now), Mike was a good guy!

The Old Stone Bridge Ain't What She Used To Be

Back before our government started building the Interstate Highway System there were roads that had been used since Colonial times that had become our local highways over time. New England has many roads like this, since it was settled much earlier than other areas in our country. One of those byways became a numbered state road called Route 138.

Route 138 was originally a trail that led from Boston to the south, eventually leading to Newport, Rhode Island, another Colonial-era seaport. The road meandered through towns and cities like Canton, Stoughton, Taunton and Fall River in Massachusetts and then crossed into Rhode Island, making its way to Newport. Like many cities in New England, these towns grew and prospered as a result of this primary trade route.

If you've ever seen a map of Rhode Island, you'll quickly understand why it's called *The Ocean State*. Narragansett Bay and its estuaries and rivers give this tiny state an incredible amount of waterfront property, not to mention a ton of angling opportunity. So to continue Route 138 into Newport, a bridge had to be constructed across the Sakonnet River, on the east side of Narragansett Bay.

The history of the crossing goes back to 1640, when

a ferry across the river was established; the first wooden bridge was started in 1794, but wasn't in full use until 1810. The state built a new stone bridge in 1907, which serviced the Route 138 traffic until closing in 1956. I'm not exactly certain as to the year it was decided to demolish the channel (central) portion of the old bridge, but the result was pier-like access for fishing from both sides of the river.

At some point in the mid-seventies, while I was fishing the Cape Cod Canal with my other friends, I began to spend some nights parked on the old bridge with one of my neighbors, who had been fishing there a couple times. The main attraction at the bridge was a fish the locals called squeteague. This fish, identified by its Indian name in Rhode Island, is known to the rest of the world as weakfish. It's also referred to as gray trout, summer trout and tide runner.

Squeteague love squid, and they follow the summer squid runs throughout Narragansett Bay. We caught them using bottom rigs much like a flounder rig. The rig consisted of a 3-ounce weight usually, with two leaders running off the main line. Both hooks would be set up with squid strips or heads, and then tossed out to await the fish. There was enough current to keep the strips undulating in the water, which made it pretty easy for us.

The average size was probably between eight and twelve pounds; the Rhode Island state record is nineteen pounds. The meat was white and grilling or broiling it seemed to be the best method for cooking it. I can't say the fish was exciting to catch; it didn't have the fight that stripers and blues offered, but the whole bridge thing made it worthwhile. It was a night out fishing, and that's never bad!

The fun thing about the bridge was the easy access; I

could drive my van out to the end, grab the best available spot and back in. I'd open the back doors to access our gear, and we'd set up lawn chairs and coolers in minutes. There wasn't any walking for a mile; this was a lazy man's game. You'd bait up, cast out, set your rod against the old steel railing and sit down and enjoy the evening. We got to know all the regulars, so we'd share stories and beers until the fish showed up. Sometimes they didn't, but we still had a good time.

One of the most difficult things to deal with on the bridge was getting your fish up to the deck. When we first started fishing there, the norm was using a stiff rod and heavy line that would allow you to pull the fish up. But like any other species of trout, squeteague have a soft mouth, which made it quite difficult to get them to the rail. We watched a lot of fish fall back into the water as the hook ripped out of their mouth, which certainly wasn't good.

Some of the guys had tried making long-handled gaffs, but they weren't the best alternative, either, so we ended up walking our rods back down the bridge, where we'd go onto the beach, and with any luck manage to bring our fish in. I have never liked over-gearing for a fish; I tend to go with a lighter rod, reel and line combination to keep it a little sportier, so horsing it in wasn't an alternative for me.

My friend Larry felt the same way; our tackle was not a match for the conditions. One night, when I picked him up he threw his gear into my truck. I noticed he had a big, flat plastic bread tray, the kind that bakeries use to transport their goods. The bright red tray was full of rope.

Of course I asked him what that contraption was all about, and all he'd tell me was if his idea worked, he wouldn't have to listen to me bitching anymore. I gave him that one, and waited patiently to find out what he was up to. The tray was in the back of my van when one of the guys we knew hooked up with a nice fish. As he was about to start walking off the bridge, Larry told him to stay where he was; he had a little surprise for us all. He told the guy to get it in close below the rail and let him do the rest.

As the fish started getting in close, Larry grabbed the bread tray, unfurling the ropes as he went. He had tied a length of rope to each corner and connected them to a large O-ring, onto which he tied the drop rope. He leaned over the rail and dropped the tray down into the water. He maneuvered it to slide underneath the fish, and then he pulled it out of the water and up onto the bridge. He had attracted a lot of attention, and the guys on the bridge got pretty excited about his new invention.

Larry wasn't completely satisfied, though. He said it had been hard to get the plastic tray deep enough to get under the fish, so he pulled out his tackle box and grabbed four three-ounce egg sinkers. He tied one on each corner of the tray, and then dropped it back down into the water. It sunk perfectly, as he had suspected it would. Within a couple of weeks, the bread tray recovery system was in full use at the Old Stone Bridge; most of the regulars made their own and used them all the time. If somebody didn't have one, most of the guys would land the fish for him. Human ingenuity!

One night on the bridge we heard a lot of noise coming towards us in the water. A large school of pogies was making its way towards the bridge, and it was being blown apart by hungry blues. As they approached, Larry boldly announced to us all he could land a bluefish with the silver foil wrapper in his cigarette package. He bet five dollars with any taker, and had about six gamblers who thought he was wrong.

He went to his tackle box and grabbed a good-sized hook, some split shot and duct tape. He fashioned the foil into a streamer, wrapped some tape around it and the hook, and squeezed a few split shot on the line. Everyone moved from the best spots on the outside to let him get as close as he could to the blues moving into the channel in front of us.

He threw his *lure* out a few times with no response, but on his last effort he connected. The bluefish hit the foil with a vengeance and Larry brought him up to show off. It was about five or six pounds; a decent fish, not huge, but big enough to win him thirty dollars, and I can attest to you all that thirty dollars in those days meant something. He was a character, for sure, and, once again, he proved that a man's best tool is a roll of silver duct tape!

Although we fished the Sakonnet River for squeteague, we occasionally got lucky and picked up something we weren't planning on. One night, just to change it up a bit, we decided to fish at a tank farm about a mile north of the bridge; somebody had told us that squeteague were showing up around the docks there once in a while.

The area was lined with boulders along the shoreline, so we set up our rigs and cast them out. Sticking our rods into the rocks, we settled into a couple of comfortable spots and started talking. We went almost two hours with nothing but the breeze moving our rods. We felt like the suggestion to fish there might not pan out the way we had hoped.

But, as all good fishing stories go, things changed. We had been gabbing for so long, I hadn't noticed my rod tip bouncing at all until my rod flew out of the rocks and headed for the water below. I jumped up as fast as I could (I was faster in those days; I would have lost it if it was last year) and jumped at my rod. I tripped in the rocks and went down hard, but managed to grab the butt and hold on.

I struggled to my feet and started reeling. I was sore everywhere, but the adrenaline kicked in and I got control. I knew immediately that I didn't have a squeteague because they hit bait a lot softer. I fought the fish for about fifteen minutes and landed a twenty-five pound striper.

The fish was long and lean; it was forty-two inches long and only had one squid spine in its belly when I cleaned it. Normally, a striper that long would be in the 35-40 pound range, but despite it looking like a runway model, it sure tasted good on my grill the next night!

Patience (and duct tape, of course) can sometimes be the best tool in your tackle box!

Grilled Salmon, Anyone?

I left the southeastern section of Massachusetts in the early Eighties, and moved back to my ancestral hometown of Newburyport. The small city is located about thirty miles north of Boston, and is right on the coast. It lies at the mouth of the Merrimack River, which in addition to its being one of the worst inlets on the East Coast, is a summer playground for stripers.

The river had been a striper hotspot for many years. Anglers from all over Massachusetts and nearby New Hampshire would line the beaches and jetties at its easternmost point on a small coastal sand spit called Plum Island. When the bass were running in the river, it was almost impossible to find a spot to set a sand spike in.

Sometime in the late seventies the bluefish showed up. The weather had been unusually warmer than normal, and the baitfish moved further north into the warmer water. The blues weren't far behind. They had become a fixture there every summer after that, so most of us fished with wire leaders just in case. The toothy critters just about took over as the most caught fish; it seems the bass had moved further north to dine on the bait schools there, not wanting to compete with the blues.

So even though I made many attempts to catch stripers on Plum Island, I wasn't very successful. I had picked up a few schoolies, but nothing like what I had become used to on Cape Cod. I lost interest in driving out to the Island for a couple years, and my gear got dusty until a friend of mine, who wasn't even a fisherman, called me up to tell me a story about a salmon fishing excursion he had just got back from.

He and I had become close friends for a few years, until he ran into some marital problems. After an ugly divorce he had moved up to a small town in Maine to open a pizzeria restaurant. We had lost touch during that time period; I always felt he had enough on his plate trying to start over, so we had drifted apart.

He had a guy who came into his restaurant almost every day for lunch; this guy was an avid fisherman, and was always telling Chris about his adventures. He managed to convince Chris to go with him on a salmon fishing trip on the east end of Lake Ontario in New York; three of them had gone, and my friend couldn't wait to drag me along for the next trip.

I listened to his tales of glory about landing some pretty big fish. He definitely piqued my interest, so I told him to call me in August to remind me. I thought about it through that winter and into the summer, and in August I called him and signed on. I've never regretted making that call!

Chris' buddy Mike was in charge of the expedition. He called me to tell me what I needed for the trip, and I got everything ready. He drove his van out to a small town called Pulaski, in upstate New York. It was an old mill town, but it had something going for it that not too many rundown towns could offer; three rivers running through it that were full of spawning salmon.

I'm talking thick enough to walk across salmon; there were thousands in these rivers waiting to be harvested. The fish would come into Lake Ontario and then work their way up into the rivers they were born in. The State of New York had determined that having all these fish die after spawning wasn't very prudent, so they had authorized a snagging season for harvest.

I know what you're thinking; when I first heard that we were going to be snagging these fish, I almost changed my mind. I hadn't snagged fish since I was a kid, and that was only herring in the river at the end of my street. We used to snag them and let them run all over the place before releasing them back into the water below the dam. The dam had no fish ladder, so snagging them was easy. There were hundreds of them, so it kept us amused during the spawn.

But this was salmon we were talking about; a game fish, not bait! Mike promised me I'd have fun, so I stayed on for the trip. If you've never done this before and have an opportunity to, I say *go for it* because it's worth it.

We stayed at a local guide's house; he and his family lived downstairs, and he had four bedrooms upstairs that he converted to *guest quarters*. They consisted of two sets of bunk beds and a small table in each room; there was nothing fancy. There was a big porch on the back of the house that served as our gear room, and an outdoor work station for cleaning fish if you wanted to do that yourself.

We chose to opt for the cleaning stations that were everywhere in town; they'd clean and fillet (or steak-cut) your fish, and put them in a freezer. We simply went there on our last morning, gave them our tickets and stashed the meat in our coolers. The town was set up to cater to the fishermen; restaurants had all-you-can-eat buffets, and some stayed open 24 hours during salmon season. You could walk around in your waders, and nobody gave you a second glance. It was a cool experience!

Our guide/host told us to be ready at five. He was taking us to Little Sandy Creek first; it was one of the three rivers I mentioned. After getting dressed and having something to eat, we met him downstairs. It was the first of October, and it was chilly in the pre-dawn hours. We were layered in so much clothing, with chest waders on, that I remember feeling like the *Pillsbury Dough Boy*.

When we got to the river, he parked alongside the road, where we saw a handful of other vehicles nearby. He told us not to worry about it, and that no matter where we went there was going to be a lot of competitors vying for a good spot. After rigging up with weighted treble hooks, he led us out into the water. I remember how cold my feet and legs got almost immediately, but I kept following him out into the river.

He told us there was a deep pool right in front of us, but warned us to stay in the area he was showing us. Cast into the pool; there's plenty of room, he told us. He also told us about a couple of guys who got too close to the drop-off who went under and didn't make it back out in time. I stayed right where he told me to. The deep hole was normally loaded up with salmon, stacked on top of each other for the night, and they usually started moving after first light.

It was pitch dark out there at first, but we heard a yell go out at the first sign of sunlight, and everybody started throwing their hooks in the water. We joined in; Mike was the first to hook into one, and he managed to get it in fairly quickly. It was a Chinook, the more abundant of the two species in the water; it was around twenty pounds.

Brian, our guide, was next up. His fish really fought hard, but landing salmon wasn't a new experience for him. He worked it in and put it on a rope stringer he had tied to a tree. He had set us all up with a stringer just waiting to be filled.

I cast into the pool for the fourth or fifth time, and bouncing the weighted hook, I felt something solid. I reared back and set the hook; I knew instantly that I had a fish on.

I talked about trout fishing in my earlier chapters; salmon are related to trout, so I expected the same sort of reaction from them as a trout. When I caught trout, they almost always ran upstream, so when I hooked that first salmon, I was waiting for it to break to my left. My fish dug down into the pool and ran back and forth. I could feel him bumping other fish, and thought that he'd probably cross over somebody else's line at any second.

But to my surprise, my line slackened a bit; the next thing I knew, my salmon came out of the water to my right, jumped over some rocks and took off like a bat out of hell downstream. As my drag screamed, I saw that my fish was heading into the middle of about twenty guys fishing a smaller pool.

I quickly recovered and began moving my way downstream; I thought the other anglers there would understand that this one had gotten away from me, but the screaming I heard from them was louder than that of my drag. I think I was cussed at in at least three different languages as my salmon ran right through them. Let's just say that Sister Margaret Mary would have whacked the knuckles off of every one of them for their pronouncements!

I kept apologizing to all of them as I worked my way through them, but they didn't seem to care. The insults and epithets continued to fly until I saw a guy wade out and net my fish. He held it up and told me to come and get it. When I got to him, I thanked him profusely for his assistance, but he wasn't having any of it. With a hard look, he gruffly told me to take my fish and get the f--- out of everybody's way!

And I did; by that time it was pretty light out, so I found a path that led back to my original spot, dragging my fish behind me. It was a good one, and I was anxious to weigh it. After taking a beating from everybody along the way, including my friends, I made it back to the tree where our stringers were tied. Brian met me there, and had a scale ready to go.

My catch was a Chinook that weighed in at thirty-two pounds. Even though the fish had embarrassed me, it was still good to tie her onto my stringer. She was my first, and ended up being the biggest one I caught in our three days. I added a twenty-one pound Coho the next day fishing in the Salmon River. Brian told us that a Coho that size was a great fish; it proved to be a better tasting fish, as well, I'd found out later.

On the morning of our fourth day we went to the cleaning station and picked up our fish. We each had around a hundred pounds of fillets and steaks to take home. As I mentioned, Chris owned a restaurant, so his special the following week was broiled salmon and baby red potatoes. I think Mike gave him some of his, too, but I got home and stopped by to see several friends and family members, giving each of them two or three pounds. One of my buddies called me "Salmon Claus" and our group got a kick out of that.

When I got done spreading good will, I put the rest of the salmon into my chest freezer in the basement. We ate a lot of salmon over the next few weeks, but it didn't seem to even make a dent in the supply. Not wanting to risk losing any of it to freezer burn, I told my wife that I was going to grill salmon for dinner one night every week until it was gone.

So throughout the winter I fired up my grill, grabbed a beer and stood out on my deck cooking dinner. I lived in a very cold area, known for excessive snowfall, but not once did I let that deter me from my mission. My neighbors would see me standing outside, in freezing cold or with snow blowing all around me, and think I was crazy. I'm a fisherman; I'm pretty sure I was!

Could I Have a Room With a View, Please?

In March of 1995 I moved to Sebastian, Florida. I lived in a few different places, but in 1999 I rented a small, three room cottage on US Highway 1 in Micco, just a few miles north. The house was close to the road, so traffic noise could be a problem sometimes. But the back of the house is why I chose to live there.

Ninety-five per cent of the back wall was glass, offering a view of the Indian River Lagoon, less than a hundred feet from my deck. The deck was the length of the little house, and served as an additional *outdoor* living area for most of the year. I could stand at my kitchen sink watching the nearby water and actually see redfish *tailing* in the shallows at the end of the grass. Within seconds I could grab a pre-rigged rod and be casting into the water.

My place shared a common yard with two other cottages, one on each side of the property, perpendicular to the water. We were all living there for the view, and the price was right at the time. Of the four of us that shared the property, I was the only one who fished, so I never had to worry about being crowded out.

I hadn't fished much in the first few years I lived in Florida, primarily because I didn't know a thing about fishing the flats, or catching whatever was in there. When I moved into the cottage that all changed.

I was working for a Yellow Pages directory that covered the local market. Two of the other salesmen I had befriended were interested in fishing and one of them, Phil Combass, had grown up in Florida and knew everything there was to know about fishing in the Lagoon. The three of us became fast friends after I moved into the cottage; we used to wade out onto the flats behind my house several evenings each week.

Phil taught Dave Higgins (our other friend) and me what we needed to be successful. He showed us how to use a cast net, and what bait worked best for what. Before too long, we were all catching sea trout, the mainstay back then, on a regular basis, and occasionally someone would pick up a redfish.

One night I found myself alone at my place. Phil and Dave were both doing something else that night, but the constant echo of trout smashing bait out back was too much for me to pass up. I took my rod, already rigged with a small jig head and curly-tail plastic lure and started wading out into the grass flats. Trout were popping everywhere, and I managed to hook up pretty steadily for an hour or so.

It was starting to get dark, but I could hear the trout working out a little further, so I decided to keep wading. Settling onto a solid grass clump about two hundred feet from shore, which was less than four feet deep, I continued pitching my plastics.

There was no moon at all that night, and by nine it was pretty dark out there. The Indian River isn't really a river that flows like most; it's a flatwater estuary with very little tide or current when you get away from the inlets. When the wind dies down at night, there's almost no movement in the water; it's dead calm.

Standing there casting the clock nine-to-three, I felt a very large splash of water against my legs. I froze.

The next thing I knew, I was flying across the top of the water, barely touching it as I went. I couldn't get to the shore fast enough, and continued running until my feet hit solid ground!

Just kidding! When I told my friends this story the next day, I told it just like this. The incident was dubbed my *Jesus* moment; the night I walked on water! Excuse me for being a bit blasphemous here, but it's an appropriate description. I **wanted** to run across the water because I wasn't sure where the big rush of water had come from.

You see, my house was about a quarter of a mile north of where the San Sebastian River flows into the Lagoon. The San Sebastian is famous for its big gators, and also for some very large sharks that go up in the river chasing the tarpon schools that live there. Some of those big gators move into the Lagoon when the water level is low like it was then, as the salinity levels drop quite a bit.

So when I felt the rush of water, my mind flew to sharks and gators. I did freeze; that part's true. I couldn't see any-thing, and I just held my breath hoping my visitor was not interested in dining on me. For what seemed like minutes (but was probably only ten seconds), I heard a splash and a grunt to my left about ten feet away. I just barely could make out the square-shaped head of a manatee before it went under again. I let my breath out, and unclenched my body.

I gathered what I had left of my dignity and waded back

to shore. I made a solid decision to never wade at night anymore; after that, I fished from my neighbor's dock once the sun went down. Since I wasn't tramping around in the water, I ended up catching a lot of fish from that dock, so it all worked out.

My target fish had become snook, a rare combination of speed and power that is one of South Florida's premier attractions. It hits like a train, runs like a greyhound and fights like a bluefish. The wily snook had eluded me for the first few months, until Phil decided that our best chance for snook was to stay out of the water and let the fish come to us.

As I mentioned, my neighbor next door had a nice dock with an attached boathouse. He had told me that it was fine with him if we fished from his dock as long as we cleaned up after ourselves. Phil and I set up our rods with a free-lined pinfish, one of the more common baits in our area. Phil had grabbed the biggest of the pins; it was as big as my hand. I thought it was too big, but he hooked it up and told me his theory. "The bigger the bait, the bigger the fish" he said. Acknowledging that he was probably right, we threw our baits out and sat down to see what happened.

As we were talking, Phil jumped up, kicked off his shoes and slipped off the end of the dock. It was only about three feet there, so he wasn't in any danger of going under. His rod was doubled over, and he was following the fish wherever it led him. After a few minutes he got control of the fish and walked it back in to the little beach in my yard.

It was a snook and it was beautiful; it was thirty inches long and probably about ten pounds. I couldn't help laughing at him for his swan dive off the dock, but the reward was well worth it. It was legal season for snook, so we decided to keep it and grill it up, since I had never eaten it before. For those of you who haven't tried it, I suggest doing so if you get a chance. It's a firm, white meat that has a very nice flavor; I've always grilled it with lemon and melted butter, but I've had it fried in a light batter and it was equally delicious.

Phil's *kamikaze* dive off the dock had inspired me. I saw the excitement on his face his catch had generated, so I made it my mission to become a snook fisherman. I've caught quite a few over the years, and they always put up a tough fight, regardless of their size. They're a lot of fun to catch!

The following summer I had a different kind of experience on the dock. It was a warm Friday night, and my neighbor was having a little get-together. I joined his group for a hamburger and a beer, but after dark I made my way out onto the dock.

I'd been out netting finger mullet earlier and had a bucket full. I was still wearing my wading booties; they were soft-sided with hard rubber soles for walking on shells or rock. They fit like slippers, so rather than changing into sandals, I had just left them on while I was eating.

I set up a lawn chair, rigged my bait and tossed it out. I was free-lining, and several times my line ran out and I set the hook on what proved to be a fat catfish. I was getting pretty frustrated; catfish have never been my fish of choice. This saltwater species is considered a nuisance fish; they're not anything I'd ever eat and they're a pain in the butt! I kept cutting my line to release the nasty things, having to rig up again each time.

By eleven I had caught about twelve cats, with no sign

of a trout or a snook. I was past frustrated at this point; they were wiping out my mullet supply, and I was getting pissed off at these ugly critters. The party had broken up by then, and my neighbor and his girlfriend had walked out on the dock to see how I was doing.

We sat around chatting for almost an hour before they went back into the house. I resumed my fishing, hoping that the catfish had left town. Within a couple minutes, my line was running pretty fast. I waited until the fish slowed down and set the hook. Thinking it was a trout at first, I realized as soon as the fish started running that I had another catfish on my line.

I dragged it up on the dock and cut the line. I pushed it aside with my knife, thinking it would fall back into the water, but it was just lying there looking stupid. That's when I did my best *Ray Guy* impression and punted that fish right off the dock.

Pain shot up my leg instantly; I sat down and took my bootie off, thinking I might find a barb sticking out. Unable to see much out there, I limped back to Tom's house and asked for help. His girlfriend got some hydrogen peroxide and a pair of tweezers, but she couldn't find anything. She did manage to open up the wound enough to get it bleeding pretty well, but found no barb.

So she bandaged me up, and I went back out on the dock and fished until two. The cats seemed to have moved out, so I actually ended up catching a couple of trout before calling it a night.

My wound wasn't healing very well. Playing the *macho* angle, I had decided to let it get better on its own, but it wasn't working. After a golfing trip to North Carolina with

Phil and Dave, I came home with my toe throbbing with pain, so I went to the Emergency Room at our nearby hospital.

The next morning I was back there for *Outpatient Surgery*. X-rays had shown that I had something wedged into the joint bones of my big toe. They put me out, removed a serrated barb about a half-inch long and stitched me up.

After I came down from the anesthesia later that afternoon they sent me home. A nurse gave me a little plastic bag with the barb in it; she jokingly said that she thought I should keep this to remind me of how foolish I had been.

I received a bill from the hospital a couple weeks later. The total cost of my *being foolish* was eighteen thousand dollars! Thankfully, my insurance paid most of it, but I was left with a balance of around five hundred dollars. Foolish? No; completely stupid! I still have that barb to this day, and I promise you I've never kicked another catfish!

Boat Stories

Every angler I know is convinced that having a boat will automatically increase your odds of catching fish. I can't argue with that reasoning; having a boat does allow you to move around a lot more until you locate some willing fish. But every one of us who owns, or who has owned, a boat will tell you that sometimes the advantages don't always outweigh the disadvantages one encounters when you own one.

Favorite lines like "BOAT – Bring On Another Thousand" or "a boat is a hole in the water one throws money into" are heard coming from the mouths of every boat owner I've ever met. But my favorite is "A boat owner's favorite two days are the day you buy one and the day you sell it." I've owned two boats over the years here in Florida; I'm currently unencumbered by boat ownership and have been for several years.

There are always some humorous stories when you own a boat. My first boat was a seventeen-foot center console. It was a perfect boat for fishing in the Indian River Lagoon, and I worked it hard. I spent a lot of time with Phil Combass in this boat; David Higgins had moved up to Georgia by then and was out of the picture.

One morning after I first got the boat, Phil and I arrived at the ramp, loaded everything up and took off. The Lagoon is quite wide, but not very deep. When we were just about in the Intracoastal Waterway channel, I turned around and noticed my stern was almost under water. I had to make a quick decision to go back to the dock, or head to a spoil island out in front of us.

I realized that I had forgotten the plug! I cranked up the motor, got her up on plane and headed for the island. Once the boat was on plane, the water level in the boat started to drop. The bilge pump was going, but it was struggling to keep up. With a sandy beach in front of me, I pointed the bow into it and grounded the boat.

I shut the motor down and jumped out. The plug had been rolling around on the deck, so I grabbed it and waded into the water. The stern was in about three feet of water, and the drain hole wasn't quite reachable, so I had to dive under to find it. I got the plug in, but spent the next few hours soaking wet on a very cool morning. A lesson learned, but definitely not fun!

Another day Phil and I were out fishing for four or five hours with absolutely nothing to show for it. Telling him I was going to try one more spot that had given up some tailing redfish on several previous visits, we moved from one spoil island to the next, but still had nothing in the box. While making our way over some grass flats en route to another island, I had a strange occurrence.

Phil was sitting up front, watching for some signs of life, and I was moving the boat in very slowly. As I was about to shut the engine down for a drift, something hit me in the butt. I turned around and couldn't believe what was flopping around on my deck.

There was a very nice pompano behind me jumping all over the place! Pompano aren't big fish, but this one was big enough to get a couple nice fillets, which I grilled up later and made two great sandwiches out of. Apparently, some predator was chasing the pomp when he decided to jump into the boat. Little did he know at the time he was literally jumping from the fire into the frying pan!

As I told the story to Phil, I remember telling him that this must be God's way of helping a couple of sorry-ass fishermen get a bite to eat. He must have been looking down saying "I think I'm going to hit that guy right square in the shorts." That's my story, and I'm sticking to it.

Another time we were out by the Sebastian Inlet, drifting with the incoming tide. It was flounder season, so we were bouncing live finger mullet off the bottom. Mullet and mud minnows are the baits of choice for flounder here in the cooler months. We were on the north side of the channel, west of the bridge.

We were in perfectly clear ocean water about fifteen feet deep. The flounder had evaded us, and once again it was not looking good. I had checked my mullet to make sure it was still alive and had thrown it back out. Standing on the stern deck waiting for my bait to settle in, I looked down into the water below us.

There was a very large shark swimming just below the boat. I estimated that it was at least ten feet long, maybe more. As you might remember, I was driving a seventeen-footer. It was a *Jaws* moment for me! We pulled our lines out and quickly moved to a different spot.

In 2004, the East Coast of Florida experienced two major hurricanes in a three week period. The effects of these two storms really wiped us out! The center console had been traded for a twenty-one foot walk-around cuddy before the bad weather, and once the Coast Guard announced that the channels were clear, we all started going fishing again.

The new boat didn't get into the shallow spots like my previous one did, but the comfort level was much higher. I had gotten used to where I could go with her, so it all balanced out nicely over time; fishing in the deeper waters around the Inlet, or just offshore became the norm.

Most days, while returning from the Inlet, I would go around the west end of the State Park, staying in the channel before cutting right to go home. There was always enough water for my boat, and I had driven through that area dozens of times before.

Not taking the Coast Guard's warnings into account on my first trip out after the hurricanes, I made my usual pass through the west end and turned westward as usual. The boat was up on plane and was starting to get some speed when the boat and I were unceremoniously stopped in our tracks. My boat was up on a sandbar that wasn't normally that far south; the storms had caused a shifting of the sandbar to about twenty feet over from where it had always been, and my boat was stuck high and dry.

After almost blowing my engine up, I shut it down and climbed out of the boat. I was alone that day (of course!), so it was up to me to try to get the boat off the bar. My port side was still in the water, although not very much. Rocking her sideways, then front and back for a few minutes, I actually could feel the boat starting to shift off the sand, but I still had a way to go before I could get back in.

I had mentioned in an earlier story that the Indian River Lagoon has virtually no tides except around the inlets. As I pushed and cajoled the boat, it started to move very quickly. The tide was coming in from the ocean, and the wind was blowing out of the northeast. That combination was what made it possible for me to get my boat out of the mud and back into deeper water.

The only drawback to this was the fact that the ladder on my swim platform was on the port side; I was standing on the sandbar on the starboard side. When the boat started moving fast, I made an attempt to grab the ladder and climb back on board. I wasn't successful. My feeble grasp wasn't quick enough, and I ended up in the water trying to hold on.

The wind and tide continued pushing my boat towards the south. I was hanging onto the ladder trying to get a foothold, but I couldn't do it. As a crowd onshore looked on, my boat was blown across the deeper water into shallow grass flats, where I finally managed to climb onboard. I had a pole onboard to help out in these situations, and used it to push myself out of the grass and get back underway.

The crowd roared! They loved every minute of it; they were fishing from shore, and here I was, struggling to get my dumb ass back into the boat. I'm sure they all went home and told that story to all their friends; it was that pathetic!

I sure loved my boats!

Marlin Memories

If you were to ask me what type of angler I am, the answer would be an inshore guy. I'm most comfortable on the flats here in Florida, whether in a boat or on dry land. When up north, I was always fishing from beaches, rocks and jetties or wading in tidal rivers. It's where I'm most comfortable, and it's definitely where the majority of my fish have been caught throughout my life.

I have friends who go offshore several times a month and rave about the dolphin, cobia, kingfish and grouper they catch. I'm not saying this isn't fun; I've been on quite a few offshore trips and really enjoyed them without ever being seasick, no matter what, so that's not a problem. It's just that I happen to like my feet on the ground when a fish hits; it's just a personal preference.

That being said, I have had two opportunities in my lifetime to go marlin hunting, with tremendous memories from each of the trips. Going two for two on these excursions puts me into some good company, from what I hear. Believe me, there's something to be said for seeing a fish seven or eight feet long on the end of your line jumping magnificently out of the water.

It's an absolute thrill, for sure! I had always thought about getting a chance to fish for big game like marlin, so I was lucky to make the best of both opportunities. Here's what happened that enabled me to live, not one, but two experiences of a lifetime.

I worked in sales and management for a Yellow Pages Directory for ten years. Winning my company's President's Club Award for my sales performance in 2005 afforded me the first chance at a marlin. That year all of the people chosen for this award were given a trip to Cabo San Lucas, Mexico, in the Mexican Baja, along with a thousand dollars each to spend on anything we wanted to.

I was still playing golf when we made the trip in May of 2006, so one of my choices for that week was teeing it up on a seaside course designed by Jack Nicklaus. The cost was $250 for an eighteen hole round, something I wouldn't even dream about doing in Florida. The course ate me alive, but the layouts and the scenery really made it all worthwhile. Turning a corner and emerging from thick scrub into a hillside tee box that had an incredible view of the Pacific Ocean smashing the rocks below the course is permanently etched into my mind.

That same night someone started talking about an offshore fishing trip; he wanted to know how many of us would be interested. About twenty people had raised their hand, so he told us all he'd go to the marina to see if he could get us a package deal. He did pretty well, securing four boats for $250 per person. Since I'd already spent that much on golf, I signed up, more confident in my fishing abilities than golfing.

As it turned out, there were sixteen of us that actually went, so the fleet owner put us on three boats. I was on one of the larger boats and had five other people on board. We drew straws to set the chair rotation, and I was lucky enough to get the first try. After watching the Captain and his mates haggling over bait prices at a floating wholesaler, we made our way out of the harbor past the jagged rocks along the outside of the entrance.

A half-hour later, we were in twelve thousand feet of water, only a few miles offshore. We could still see the beach as the mates were rigging up rods and getting ready to fish. Our target that day was Pacific striped marlin, a beautiful quarry that was making its annual appearance there. We only trolled for about ten minutes before we had a hit on the starboard line. One of the mates reeled in the other rod, and handed me the live one. Man, I've got to tell you, it was unbelievable!

The rod was set into the fighting chair, but that fish just about pulled me and the rod right out of it. Within a couple of minutes, the marlin made its first jump. I was in awe of the big blue monster on the end of my line, but kept reeling as he jumped, not giving him a chance to break free. He dove and ran, and came up again.

The mate kept telling me to keep the line tight, so I did. Again, the fish went under and made a run right at us. As I was reeling like a madman, he suddenly made a big turn and started dragging line out faster than I could get him in. He came up for what turned out to be the last time, jumping higher out of the water than either of the other two times.

He was getting a little tired, so I made a move to bring him in by tightening down on the drag a little and reeling hard, pulling him toward me as the reel sang out. The big fish was zigging and zagging alongside the boat, but the battle was coming to a close.

The Captain yelled down from the fly bridge to ask me if I wanted a trophy. "Yes, only a trophy; just get his measurements" I yelled back, continuing the struggle to get him close. Killing this magnificent fish wasn't part of my plan; marlin isn't that tasty and we were on the other side of the country in Mexico. Expecting a standard catch-and-release, we all watched a horror show instead!

As the mates grabbed my fish at the stern, they pulled it up over the side and started beating it with a baseball bat. Blood was flying everywhere, and I was screaming at these guys like they were killing the family dog, all to no avail. They looked at me like they had no clue what I was saying, and just continued beating the marlin until it was completely lifeless.

I screamed at the Captain and asked what the hell was going on; his answer was that I wanted a trophy, so they had to kill the fish. I was pissed off because they didn't have to do that, but it was too late. The striped marlin turned out to be eight-feet long and about a hundred and twenty-five pounds. I had a replica made and that's been moving around with me ever since. It's now mounted on my porch, since it's the only place big enough to display and enjoy it. It's actually the only fish that I've had a replica made of; it was $1800 delivered!

We heard a story later that the locals kill the marlin to sell to local restaurants who make a famous smoked marlin fish dip that is served all over Cabo. So if you ever get a chance to catch a billfish in Mexico, always be sure that the Captain completely understands that you do not want your fish killed; otherwise, it may end up being an appetizer at Sammy Hagar's Cabo Wabo Cantina!

Five years later I had another chance to chase marlin; this time it was for white marlin, the pride of Virginia

Beach, Virginia. I was on the corporate staff at Coastal Angler Magazine, and was offered a four day trip to Virginia Beach by the local Chamber of Commerce. It was an all-expenses-paid trip, which included two days offshore with two very qualified and well known local captains.

As a Coastal Angler staffer, my mission was to partake of the local hospitality. Staying at a beachfront hotel, dining in nice seafood restaurants every night, and fishing is what the trip was all about. It was tough, but we managed to pull through it all. The Chamber was expecting a strong endorsement article in the National section of our magazine, obviously hyping the local amenities, which was handled upon my return. We were joined by another angler from Alabama, who had been invited to participate for the same reason.

Before I get into the story any further, let me to tell you about white marlin fishing off the shores of Maryland and Virginia. September is generally referred to as being *White Hot*, as in white marlin hot; this species invades the waters here every September, and they tear up anything the boats throw out. It's pretty wild!

One of the boats we fished on held the record for most whites in a day. With Captain Gary Richardson at the helm, his anglers caught and released one hundred and six fish on September 12, 1983. In one day! (The season total release of 266 whites is held by a boat from Ocean City, MD, just up the beach.) The other captain we went out with had just won the biggest white marlin tournament of the season. So we were definitely in good company.

The first couple of weeks of September had been smoking; twenty-five to thirty flags up on returning boats were a common sight. But by the time we got there, the bite had slowed down considerably. The crews were working hard to bring in two or three fish per day, and a lot of the boats were coming in with nothing. It wasn't quite over, but it was almost done.

We set out at five both mornings. The captains had to drive about two and a half hours before the lines were even put in the water. We averaged around seventy-five to eighty miles offshore each day. They would look for large eddies of warmer water that had spun off the Gulf Stream. Huge bait pods would follow these pockets, and the white marlin followed them.

These warm spots had begun to break up, and as they did the bait pods left to find warmer water somewhere else. The whites and dolphin had gone with them, moving further south, so we didn't get a lot of rises or hook-ups on our first day out. I had the only shot at a white that day, and it broke me off on a huge jump. That was it for the day.

Alan, my fishing partner, and I each got a chance the next morning, but we both lost our fish. The captain moved off to a different area and we started again. A short time later, he began yelling to the mates about rises on two of the lines, and one of them turned into a strike.

Alan was given the rod, since it was his turn. As he began the fight, the other line was hit hard and the mate handed it to me. We were in separate corners of the aft deck, and our fish were going crazy. As I attempted to get mine under control, Alan's fish took off in the same direction.

We had both fish leaping out of the water almost on top of each other. That's never good, and I took the hit on a double jump. My fish broke off, but Alan was hanging on with his. He landed it at the stern, and the mate checked the size and cut the fish loose. He called it out as being about 74 inches and forty to fifty pounds. It was, according to the captain, about the average size of what they'd been catching throughout August and September.

We failed to bring anything else up in that area, so once again the captain took off for another area. Along the way we were entertained by a large pod of bottlenose dolphins. They were doing all kinds of stunts as they swam alongside the boat; they stayed with us for about fifteen minutes and then swam off.

By that time, we had reached the spot where we would start fishing again. The lines were dropped in, and we sat back and waited for some action. There was a question of whose turn it was, but Alan deferred to me, since he'd already been able to land one. I was rewarded very soon after we started trolling.

Once again the captain announced a rise on one of the baits; I strapped on the belt and got ready. The white poked at the bait five or six times before deciding to smash it, which he finally did. Once hooked, the mate turned it over to me and challenged my manhood by telling me I had to land this one, since I had already lost a pair. "It's your time" he screamed at me.

Remembering my experience with the striped marlin I'd caught in Mexico, I made sure I was braced when I took the rod, setting the butt into my belt and hauling back, reeling as I did. The fish flew out of the water in a wild jump. The mate yelled out that it was a big one, and I just kept reeling. The marlin was definitely winning the battle; line was peeling off the reel like there was an everlasting supply of it on there, but I knew there wasn't.

It was important to get some of the line back; the captain saw my predicament and started backing the boat down to help out. The fish kept coming up, one terrific aerial after another, and I kept reeling. Part of the problem was the rod and reel; if you remember, the average fish had been around forty pounds, but this fish was bigger. It was testing every ounce of the medium weight gear.

The fish was jerking the rod out of the belt so much I finally just tucked it under my arm and reeled as hard as I could. With the captain's help, we finally managed to turn that fish around and get him swimming towards the boat. As he came up at the stern the mate confirmed his earlier appraisal. "It's a big one, Captain; must be eighty pounds!"

That was music to my ears. I no longer felt like a candy-ass fisherman who couldn't land a fish without the captain backing the boat down. The mate added that it was right around 84 inches, which was a nice fish, and that made me feel even better. I even heard the captain talking to another boat telling the captain on the other end that we had brought up an eighty-pounder.

Due to the lighter tackle, the fight for the marlin lasted almost forty minutes. When I got done, I was whipped! The downside to this trip was realizing at age sixty-two that fishing for smaller quarry was a better plan for the future; my big fish days were over!

My Grandson Casey

My son Sean took full custody of his young son when he was five years old. Casey had lived with his mother before that, but circumstances changed and Fate brought a young boy into our lives who continues to warm the hearts of everyone in my family. Casey became a very special member of the Bradbury family; a status he still enjoys with all of us.

He's sixteen now, a sophomore in high school who's growing taller by the minute. He's a young man, with a whole different set of interests, but he's still a great kid. My son, who had lost interest years earlier, had never taken him fishing, so two and a half years ago I bought him a round-trip ticket to Florida, promising to teach him how to fish.

He was thirteen then, and like most kids his age, he spent way too much time sitting in front of a computer or a game box playing video games. He was good, but I clued him in that there was real stuff in the real world that was more fun. It was time to experience some of that!

The first morning he was here we went across the street to a friend's dock. You've heard me mention jig heads and plastic tails before; this was what my tackle bag was full of. I could usually wade out anywhere in the Indian River lagoon and hook up with something on my jigs, so they always got a lot of use. I probably use about twenty different colors and tail shapes, but the bottom line is I get results with jigs.

So I rigged up a jig for him and showed him how to cast the rod. I explained the process and let him go. He practiced a few casts, and then got slammed by a hungry sea trout. He damned near fell off the dock in his excitement! He had the most serious, life or death look on his face as he reeled the fish in.

In his haste to land it, he lost it about ten feet from the dock. Telling him to be a little more patient, I loosened the drag on the reel and told him to cast in a different direction. I explained that he shouldn't try to horse the fish in by ripping it out of the water; staying cool was a better plan.

He cast a few more times before he got another aggressive strike. This time he followed my directions; he took his time and a few minutes later he landed a nice trout about sixteen inches. It was his first fish! He was pumped; he was trying not to look like an excited little boy, but he wasn't doing a good job with that. Like Fred Lounsbury had done to me fifty years before, I had successfully set the hook on a new life of fishing adventures.

We kept fishing for a couple more hours; it was August and it was hot. The bite tailed off, so we headed home for some lunch. We spent the day hanging out, getting to know each other a little better. It was our first time as just the two of us outside of a couple hours here and there prior to his trip, so we were both looking forward to our time together.

The next morning we went back out to the dock. The action was as fast as the day before; we both caught a bunch of trout and an occasional puffer fish. The puffers love to chase plastic baits and bite them in half. I've had to change out at least a couple hundred tails, if not more, over the years thanks to these pesky little things, so like the previous story about catfish, I have about the same amount of disdain for them as the cats. But unfortunately, they're both part of the ecosystem in our Lagoon and they have their roles to play, so we all have to put up with them.

The following evening I decided to introduce him to snook fishing. We ate an early dinner and headed out to one of my favorite snook holes. This spot is usually lights out on an outgoing tide; several predator fish like to hang out in this hole, waiting for the huge bait schools that come out of the creek on the outgoing. I've caught just about every type of predator here, including a three foot shark.

I took a heavier action rod this time and set him up with one of my older UglyStix rod and reel combos. We rigged up with my jigs, as always, but this time I used a root beer curly tail. We were the only ones around that night, which was pretty unusual, so we pretty much could cast anywhere.

We started picking up fish right away. We caught several nice trout and a couple of flounder (Casey caught a nice one), but there wasn't any sign of a snook. As it started getting a little darker, and the tide started running lower, the bait started jumping all over the place. I knew as soon as we heard the pops that it was snook. They had moved in.

The finger mullet were so dense there that it was almost impossible to get the snook to notice our baits. I switched over to a mullet imitation on my jig and waited for the right time. It didn't take long.

There was a monster swirl and a big splash in the center of the bait pod. I cast into the ripples, hoping to get the big fish's attention. I did. The fish hit my jig like a freight train, and started peeling line off my reel like it was leaving town. I walked into the water, following the fish as my buddy Phil had taught me years before. It was about 100 feet offshore, running on a parallel line to the shore.

The fish never came up; it plowed through the water despite my best efforts to turn it. I walked along with it for about fifty feet before I had my broken line come zinging back at me. It was a crushing blow; my grandson had gotten seriously excited by the action, and there was nothing to show for it. "We'll come back tomorrow night and get him" I promised, and we gathered up our gear and headed home.

We did go back to that spot the next night, but this time I waited until it got a little closer to dark before starting. As it was the night before, the action was all around us. We started casting into the schools hoping for another shot. I wanted Casey to get his chance with a snook, but deep down I really wanted to get the one that got away the night before.

I saw a huge splash off to my right; bait scattered in every direction, running away from whatever was in there chasing it. I waited for the water to calm down a bit, and then cast into the same area. My bait got slammed instantly!

The fish ran hard and fast away from me into deeper water. Not wanting to disrupt everything by wading in after it like I had done the night before, I stayed on the beach and fought the fight. He got the drag screaming, and I reeled the line back in. This went on for about ten minutes before he started coming my way.

I've caught a lot of snook over the years, so I knew that this was a big one. I use braided line now, with a twenty-pound fluorocarbon leader, but I thought sure that wasn't going to be enough for this fish. Visions of losing it like the one the night before flashed through my head, so I backed off a little and let it get tired. The strategy paid off!

It was coming in, and it was becoming obvious that I'd get it to shore without losing it. The fight was over; I just needed to stay calm and bring it in easy up onto the sand. Casey was standing nearby waiting to see what it was that had been giving me so much trouble. After a little tussle when the water got shallow, I was able to walk it up onto the beach.

We were both shocked! We were looking at a very large, fat snook. I grabbed my tape and measured it at 38 inches. I didn't have a scale with me, so I don't know how much it weighed, but thought it was probably close to twenty pounds. Flipping the hook out of its mouth with my de-hooker, I walked it back into the water, swirling it around a little to get it revived. The fish got a second wind and we watched it swim off, as my grandson stared at me like I had three heads.

"Grampa, why did you let that fish go? It was huge; couldn't we eat it?"

I just laughed and sat down to explain catch-and-release fishing, and why so many anglers practice it most of the time. I told him about the slot limits of 28"- 32" and added that the most important reason was because snook season was closed to harvest. It was illegal to take a snook in August, since that was one of the spawning months, so keeping it was out of the question even if it was in the slot. I still wonder if he understood all that, but he seemed to at the time.

Near the end of his visit we went back to the same place to give it another try. He had been catching trout pretty regularly, but he hadn't had any luck with a snook. As usual, the bait fish were everywhere, but the tide was wrong. Still thinking it might be worth the gamble, I took a shot.

We had each picked up a couple of small trout when I saw a huge bait pod coming right at us. It was still a ways off, but the school was being hammered by some big fish. It seemed to be a large tarpon school, following the bait down the river. I told Casey to put his rod into a rock crevice and get ready. As the bait got closer, I was able to send my jig flying right into it. As soon as it hit the water, a tarpon exploded on it. Setting the hook, I handed my rod to Casey, telling him to keep the rod tip down and to keep reeling until I told him to stop.

He barely had the rod in his hands when the fish came out of the water. It was about thirty inches long and probably around fifteen to twenty pounds. His eyeballs almost literally popped out of his head! I'll never forget the look on his face every time that tarpon came out of the water; it's a priceless memory!

The tarpon jumped a total of five times before finally breaking the line. Casey kept reeling, just like I had told him to, but he knew it wasn't the same. He looked over at me with a long face and said "I think I lost it, Grampa."

I couldn't stop laughing. I finally composed myself and assured him he was only one of thousands who had the same experience with a tarpon, especially the first time. The best part of the whole event was that he got to feel what it's like to have a gamester on his line. He still talks about it.

Honorable Mention

A Few Scattered Tidbits...

Fishing was a personal obsession for me in the late Sixties; I loved it, and spent a great deal of time trying to learn everything available about the different aspects of it. An older friend of mine was an avid fly fisherman, and he loved to tell me about his fly fishing adventures, so at his urging, I decided to try it.

Spending an entire week's pay on a fly rod and reel, line, tippets and a small assortment of flies and bugs, I started practicing out in the field behind my house, until one day I thought I was ready to actually go for it at the nearby pond. My friend had told me if I ever caught a nice bass on a fly rod that I'd never go back to a spinning rod and reel. I had my doubts, but was willing and eager to give it a shot.

Making my way out to the old dam, the scene of many of my bass catches during that time, I put my rod together, tied on a popping bug, and chose a spot to begin. It was necessary to wade out a bit to get away from the shore, since it was lined with trees and brush.

Thinking I was ready, I pulled some line off my reel to begin my cast, and after working enough out to land my popper somewhere near where the fish should have been, I went for it, immediately getting hooked into a tree branch behind me, and of course as I yanked on the bug to release it, it became embedded in the branch and wouldn't let go. I broke it off and started anew.

Same thing; all my work landed me another branch on a different tree with the same results. New popper, new cast, and this time the reward was a clump of cattails behind me. I pulled my bug out of the cattails and tried again. This time I actually managed to get a cast past everything behind me, only to land in a clump of weeds fifty feet in front of me that might have been harboring a bass or two. You guessed it; by the time I got my popper out of the weeds, disturbing everything nearby, there probably wasn't a fish remaining within a hundred feet.

It was time to make a change if I was going to catch anything. Climbing down the side of the retaining wall at the bottom of the dam, I walked out onto the sluice. The water was low, so there wasn't too much coming over the dam, but there was an ample supply of algae growing on it. I made it about halfway across the dam when my feet went out from under me and I fell on my butt. It wasn't pretty!

I climbed back up, walked about twenty feet and fell again. At this point it was closer to the other side, so I kept going until I was able to climb up and find an open spot to resume my fishing. I picked out a good looking spot and went through the motions of looking like I knew what was going on, and not fooling anyone, that's for sure!

What I actually did was continue to make an ass of myself by hooking into just about every clump of cattails or weeds in the pond, effectively driving every fish in the area to places unknown. There was nothing left to hit my bug if it landed on their nose; they were gone!

It was almost dark, so I decided to call it a night. Packing up my gear, I climbed down onto the sluice and crossed over, managing to do that without falling once, having learned something from my earlier crossing.

You know what else I learned that night? Exactly; I wasn't a fly fisherman. I was a spinning rod and reel guy, and still am to this day! The next day I put a sign up at the sporting goods store offering my once-used fly rod and gear for half of what I had paid for it just two weeks before. The guy that bought it thought I did him a huge favor; he was happy as a clam (a perfect example of "one man's trash is another man's treasure")!

I've watched dozens of movies, TV shows and videos over the years extolling the virtues of fly fishing. They always make it look so easy; the line flies out with the greatest of ease, the fly lands perfectly and a beautiful trout or salmon rises to it and takes a ride. I'm pretty sure that's all an Orvis conspiracy!

Back in the Eighties I went out on a half-day charter out of Boynton Beach, Florida, with three of my friends. Boynton Beach is in Palm Beach County, where the Gulf Stream and all its wonderful fish comes as close as three miles off the beaches. Naturally, our expectations were running high, and we were all anticipating some heated action.

In the first hour, I caught a bonito about six pounds. The little bullet head was all we managed for the first three hours. My friend Greg was last up and asked the captain if he could do some deep jigging on a reef. He just wanted to put a fish in the box!

The captain obliged, and made his way to an artificial

reef close by. The mate rigged him up and dropped a big jig down to about 150 feet. As soon as it got down near the bottom Greg got a good hit. He set the hook and proceeded to fight his fish for the next forty-five minutes. The blood vessels in his head and on his arms were ready to burst. When he finally got it to the boat it turned out to be a forty-two pound amberjack.

Amberjacks are known to be warriors when it comes to landing them, but they're not considered a real sport fish. Greg didn't care; when we got off the boat he placed an order for a replica mount. The captain even tried to talk him out of it, but he went ahead and ordered it.

Greg told us then that he never worked so hard, for so long, to catch anything in his life before that and he wanted to be able to look that fish in the eye and say "I beat your ass, you ugly bastard!"

I talked much earlier about fishing for striped bass at the Cape Cod Canal. One night my buddy Bruce's kid brother came with us. Harry would join us every once in a while, but he wasn't a regular.

One night he and I were standing on a couple of rocks about fifty feet apart when Harry got hit so hard he lost his balance and almost slipped into the Canal. He regained his balance, only to listen and watch helplessly as a very big fish stripped his spool of 350 yards of seventeen-pound test in just about ten seconds!

Ziiiiiiiiiiiing, ping, and it was over! I had never seen that before, and still haven't even to this day. Harry made sure to tighten his drag up a bit when he showed up the next time!

In the fall of 2008 I was invited to participate in an inshore tournament in Stuart. Being the co-publisher of Coastal Angler at the time, I became a sponsor, thus the invite. I asked a couple of younger guys to join my team. They were both in their late twenties, and thought they were pretty good fishermen. One of them knew the local waters really well, so he drove his boat. It was an all-night event, starting at eleven and finishing up with a weigh-in at two the next afternoon.

As you might imagine, I was the brunt of some serious ass-busting. Could I make it through the night? Could I hang with the young guys? Would I be a burden to my teammates? Could somebody as old as me still fight a good snook? I got it all for a few days leading up to the tournament, but I handled it in stride.

The boys didn't know I was stocking up on sleep time, going to bed early, getting up late, and even throwing a nap or two in for good measure. And just for the hell of it, I downed a large can of Red Bull before we went out. I was ready!

We decided to fish one of the causeway bridges first. We got into some snook right away, and had a couple in the box before midnight. We got three more in the next couple of hours, for a total of five. Points were awarded by the inch for each species, and snook were double points.

We had a point total of 294 based on 147 inches of snook. Unfortunately, we didn't catch a trout, redfish or a tarpon, so we never got any other points. We came in second to a team that used two boats to go after some big over-slot redfish outside the area. They racked up about 700 points with a boatload of big reds. The tournament rules were changed the next year to disallow going out of local waters.

The daily bag limit for snook back then was two per person. We had caught five snook that night, and every one of them was in the slot. None of us had ever seen that before; there's always too small or too big, like Goldilocks, but these were all just right!

And go ahead and guess who the only man on the boat was who stayed awake until five o'clock the next afternoon. That's right; it was me, the old man. Oh, and of the five snook, three of them were caught by me. The young lads never dissed me again!

My friend Phil Combass is a guy who can catch a fish anywhere; I used to tell people that if he fished in a manhole long enough, he'd catch something! But he has a propensity for losing other things that I'll touch on for a minute.

If you grew up in the Fifties and Sixties like we did, you probably remember S & H Green Stamps. These stamps were given out by grocery stores, gas stations and tons of other businesses. After pasting them into books, you could go to one of their redemption centers and turn them in for merchandise.

In 1961, as a twelve-year old, Phil's mother gave him enough stamps to get a new rod and reel. He went down to the S&H store and traded them for a Zebco push-button spinning combo. From there he made his way to a local hardware store, bought himself some tackle and promptly went to a nearby creek that fed into the St. John's River in

Jacksonville.

He dug some clams by hand to use for bait, and hooked one up, casting it out into the creek. He wandered off for a couple of minutes, only to find that his brand-new rod and reel had vanished when he returned. Ouch!

About ten years later, after getting out of the Army, his father took him on a fishing trip on a big lake in Tennessee. It was his birthday, and his Dad had bought him a new spinning rod and reel as a gift. While in the middle of the lake, Phil set his rod down for a minute, and (you guessed it) he somehow managed to knock the rod into the water, helplessly watching as it sank to the bottom.

His father went back to the lake the next day and dredged the bottom where the rod had gone in. He was actually able to hook the rod and retrieve it, giving it back to Phil after busting his chops a little. Double ouch!

It seems to run in the family. Phil and his younger brother Wayne were out in his boat a few years ago. They were way up in the marshes off the Intracoastal Waterway in Jacksonville, fishing for redfish, when Wayne left his rod unattended. A fish hit it and pulled it right off the boat before either of them could grab it.

Phil had a spare, so they kept fishing. About an hour after losing his rod, Wayne reeled his bait in to check it and found a long piece of monofilament line attached to it. He started pulling on the line; he felt a little resistance, so he kept bringing it in. Sure enough, his rod was at the end of the line. That's called living lucky!

The moral of the story: always secure your rods, ladies and gentlemen!

My Grand Finale

Author's Note: I wrote this story a few years ago, when I was the co-publisher of the Treasure Coast (Florida) Coastal Angler Magazine. It was a feature article I'd written about a fishing trip I took one summer morning that turned out to be a very memorable trip. Please forgive the redundancies, but I've left this story pretty much as it was written. I enjoyed writing it, and I hope you enjoy reading it.

I heard the phone ringing in the outer office, but I just ignored it. I was too busy thinking about that fishing trip I was planning with my friend Bill Carter, and I knew that my secretary would get the call. I'd already told her that I wasn't taking any calls; things were going to have to take a back seat to my omnipresent fishing lust.

"It's *Life*" she yelled, more than loud enough for me, and most of the neighbors, to hear it.

"I already told you that I'm not taking any calls! I'm way too busy thinking about that next big fish that's waiting for me out there somewhere."

"*Life* said to tell you that he knows you're here; you're always here working seven days a week. So you're going to have to pick up."

"Nope, just tell him this time I'm not here; tell him I'm making plans to go fishing."

"Well, he won't take no for an answer. He said that this is about the fiftieth time that you were supposedly going fishing, but every other time he's won out, and you've stayed in the office to deal with him."

"This time it's for real. I'm going to put aside my work, and actually go fishing. I'm going to experience what a *'Fun Life'* can be!"

"Sorry, Boss, but he said to tell you that he's on the way over here, and the two of you are going to work on your magazine until it's done. He should be arriving shortly; you know that it never takes him long to get here."

She was right. *Life* came and went as he pleased around here. I couldn't shake him, no matter how hard I tried. After all, *Life* and I have been friends (maybe more like acquaintances) for nearly sixty years, and he liked to show up with his buddy, *Time*, way too much for my liking. But if I take a moment to reflect, and I guess that's what I'm doing right now, I'd have to say that *Life* and *Time* had been mostly good to me.

Fishing was something that we used to do a lot together. We had explored the streams, rivers, and lakes of Massachusetts in my youth, and had moved on to bigger fish and bigger water as we grew. Striped bass and bluefish had become our favorite targets through the Seventies and Eighties.

And then I moved to Florida in 1995. **Wow!** Fishing was different here, and *Life* and I had a lot of new experiences to savor. The grass flats of the Indian River Lagoon became our favorite place. Trout, snook, and redfish became common table fare on my deck overlooking the river. Don't get the wrong idea, here; my "deck overlooking the river" was attached to a very old, tiny little cottage with no A/C or heat that I rented. I sweated profusely in the summer (which seemed to last 8-9 months), and froze in the winter, but it <u>was</u> on the river, and fish actually *'finned'* in my back yard! *Life* and I, along with other friends we'd met along the way, used to wade the flats, or just sit out on the neighbor's dock and do nothing more than fish and enjoy each other's company.

We used to talk about getting a boat, so that we could spend more time in more places on this beautiful body of water. Finally, we did. Our first boat here in Florida was a seventeen-foot center console, with a 75 HP Mercury on it. We took that boat north to Melbourne, and south to Fort Pierce, and it seemed like we always found where the fish were hiding that day. My close friend, Phil Combass, who really taught me how to fish the Indian River, got to enjoy *Life*, too, and things were great!

Then we did what too many boaters do; we bought a bigger boat. It seems that the old adage about always wanting to move up in size comes true for many of us who later regret that decision. This time we got a 21' Walk-Around Cuddy, with a nice roomy deck that should have been perfect. It wasn't. It was too big for me to haul around with my vehicle, so I had it in a succession of marinas, from Melbourne, to Sebastian, to Jacksonville (I moved there for 6 months and hated it), and then finally back to Merritt Island. *Life* and I had found ourselves with little or no time on the new boat, and it just wasn't like the old days.

I sold that boat a few years ago, and I've been *'boatless'* ever since. I thought when I sold the boat that I would go back to the simple pleasure of fishing from the shore; wading the flats, walking the beaches, or just sitting on a friend's dock enjoying the experience. But I didn't, and *Life* had become a real pain in the butt!

I bought this great little fishing and boating magazine a year ago, after spending eleven years selling Yellow Page advertising. I love my job! I hear the greatest stories, and I get fantastic photos of fish caught, and every month I get to sit down and work my magic putting it all together. Out comes a *Coastal Angler Magazine*; people I meet tell me they love it, and how lucky I must be to get to fish all the time. What? Fish all the time? Not with *Life* breathing down my back every day!

So, back to the story; *Life* did indeed show up on schedule, and I did get my magazine completed in time to go to press. I hope that you all enjoyed my latest issue; that's what we had to finish before we went fishing. That's right; *fishing*!

At 4:30 a.m. today I woke up from a dream that I was having about fighting a very large fish. The fish was just about pulling me off the deck of the boat that I was on! One final splash at the side of the boat, and the fish was gone. The splash must have hit me in the face, because I woke up and jumped out of bed, ready to go. I drove to Fort Pierce to meet my friend Bill Carter, the co-publisher of the *Tampa Bay Coastal Angler Magazine*, and Capt. Mark Dravo, of *Y-B Normal Charters*, who fishes and guides in the Fort Pierce area.

Mark is well known for being a *big fish* guide, one who'll put you onto something that you'll remember. Bill had fished with him on Memorial Day weekend, and had caught some great fish. I was ready!

Capt. Mark had gone out at 3:30 that morning to cast

net our bait; the live wells were full of nice threadfins and pilchards, and we were heading north towards Harbor Branch, further up the river. There were about a million mullet in about two feet of water that were being blown up, so Mark positioned the boat, and we started fishing. Within ten minutes, he realized that our bait was dying in the wells, because the water temperature had gotten too high. We got out of there right away, but we ended up losing 40-50 nice baits.

Armed with the remaining bait, Mark took us to a spot between a couple of spoil islands, where we started throwing our baits into an area that was being torn up by fish in every direction. For almost an hour we got slammed by some very aggressive snook; it seemed that every bait we tossed out was getting popped, and we were landing every other fish that hit our threadfins. There were snook flying everywhere; most were under the slot size (28"), but great fun to catch and release. It was *Fish Heaven,* and we couldn't have been happier!

And then we ran out of baits. **Monster bummer!** As the fish boiled the water all around us, we watched in awe. We threw hard baits and jigs with plastic tails, but nothing would work. They were feeding on live bait, and nothing else could even get a sniff. So, with no bait, we decided we'd have to come back another day to try this spot again (and we will), but today was great!

We were standing back on the dock before nine. We thought when we had pulled out three hours before that we'd be out on the water for several more hours. It was hard to be disappointed though; we had more action in that one hour than most of us see on an all-day excursion.

But as we all stood around and talked about our amazing little adventure, I heard a familiar voice calling to me from my truck. It was *Life*; it was time to go back to work!

TURN THIS PAGE AND GET A GLIMPSE OF THE NEXT CURSE

SERPENT'S RETURN

By Mark T. Bradbury

CHAPTER ONE

Fort Pierce, Florida
April 20, 2008

"Everybody in this room knows that until we get their attention nobody's gonna give a damn about what's going on here in our harbor. We've got the US Coast Guard Station right there on the Seaway, and they don't seem too interested in stopping what's happening."

"So, what are you proposing, Jack? What can us 'little guys' do that's going to stop the rampant pollution of our Lagoon and Inlet?"

"I'm just saying that we need to do something soon, Bob, or there won't be an edible fish, crab or clam anywhere near here. It's gotta stop, and it looks like we're the ones to do it. Nobody else is stepping up; we've got to get this fixed now!"

"Jack, we all know that the government and Big Sugar are letting this happen. It's just business as usual for our politicians. They hear us complain, come and visit, then go back to Washington and sit on their collective asses. Their payday is just around the corner at the next election; Big Sugar will pour millions of dollars into their campaign war chests, and absolutely nothing will be done to change anything in the Indian River Lagoon. That's the way it works, and that's why the gates keep opening in the St. Lucie and San Sebastian Rivers, allowing millions of gallons of pesticide-filled muck into the Lagoon. I hate to say it, but all our complaining does is make a little ripple on the pond; we need a tsunami!"

"That's what I'm saying, Bob. A tsunami is exactly the sort of thing I'm talking about. We need a big bang, not a whimper; something so serious that everybody on the east coast of Florida will sit up and pay attention to."

"Shit, man, it sounds like you've got an idea that I'm not so sure is legal. Why don't you tell the rest of us what you're thinking?"

"Eco-terrorism. That's what we've got to do to bring attention to our once-beautiful water. If there's anybody interested in hearing my plan, you should stay. If you don't want to help us save our Lagoon, you should probably leave now."

Two men in the back got up to leave. Jack Baker saw them and spoke to them directly. "I understand you guys might not want to get involved in this discussion, but all of us formed this group to stop what's going on with the discharges. We all tried to do this the right way, but all we've seen from that is two years of aggravation and frustration. There's more dumping into the rivers now than there was before we got together. We're at a crossroads, guys. We either do something big or disband the group and watch our lagoon go further down the drain. That's where we are today; before you walk out of here you need to ask yourselves if you're okay with the Indian River Lagoon and the Seaway turning into one big septic tank for all the shit the government's allowing these bastards to dump. If you're not, and I don't think either of you are, you need to make the decision of your lifetime; are you in or out?"

The men paused as everyone else watched to see what they'd do. They all knew what Jack was talking about, but nobody in the room had ever dreamed it might come to something like this. But they also knew that Jack was right; it would take something more than another petition to make the politicos know how serious they were.

Both of the men who were about to leave returned to their seats. They heard what Jack had said and they knew he was right. Tom Brady, the older of the two, said 'listen, Jack, nobody here ever signed up to go to jail. We all wanted to do something that would make a difference, but eco-terrorism? Jesus, what the hell are you thinking about?"

Twelve eyes turned to Jack Baker, six men waiting to hear what he had to say.

"Everyone here should be familiar with the supply ships that run from Fort Pierce over to the Bahamas. They go back and forth carrying all sorts of supplies to the islands. It's how the Bahamas get most of their groceries and building supplies, and they leave our docks right here in Fort Pierce.

I have a friend who works down at the docks and he told me that about once a month the sugar factory out in Belle Glade ships a boatload of bulk sugar over to Nassau. They have a packaging plant near the commercial docks that packages the bulk sugar into everything from coffee packs to ten-pound bags, and they ship it all over the islands as a Bahamian product.

It's a very slick operation that they make a ton of money from. The regular monthly shipment leaves the dock next week on Tuesday. I say we have our own version of the Boston Tea Party."

"How would we do that, Jack? Will we dress up as Patriots and dump it into the Seaway?"

"No, Tom, that wouldn't be too good for the Turning Basin. We'd need to do something when the ship is out to sea. It would be pretty simple to attach an explosive device on the hull with a timer set to go off about 50 miles out. It would need to be a charge large enough to sink her, but small enough to give the crew plenty of time to evacuate the ship. There will be ample time for the Coast Guard to get out there to pull them out; there's only the Captain and four deckhands, so them getting off safely shouldn't be an issue."

"Holy Shit, Jack! Are you kidding me? A bomb on the hull? Who's going to do that?"

A tall, quiet man named Ken Lonergan stood up and said "I'm the one who'll plant the charge. I spent time with Seal Team 4 as a specialist in underwater demolition, and this job is a very simple maneuver. I can do this in my sleep, and nobody will get hurt, I promise you. Jack and I talked about this, and I think it's a helluva plan; I say let's do this!"

The five men who were out of the original loop stared back at Ken, then Jack. To a man, they couldn't believe that their little club would ever do something like this, but here it was, a plan that could work, one that could bring attention to the plight of their beloved Lagoon. Before thirty seconds had passed they all agreed to go forth with the operation; it was on!"

CHAPTER TWO

East of Fort Pierce, Florida
April 27, 2008

The Nassau Queen had left the Fort Pierce docks a couple hours before at dawn; the captain had the ship on course, and the men sat around talking and smoking. There would be plenty to do once they got into Nassau, but the ride over was always enjoyable. It was a beautiful day, with cloudless, sapphire skies, and barely a breeze across the hull. The coffee was hot, and the men chewed on some breakfast sandwiches the cook had put together for them.

Each of the crewmen had chosen to make their living on the cargo boats of South Florida. Two of them were Haitians, hard working men who had left their impoverished island to make enough money to send home to their families in Port-au-Prince. Their once proud country, part of the island of Hispaniola, was now a barren wasteland, unlike the tropical jewel it had been in their youth. Many years of poverty had forced their people to cut down just about every tree in Haiti for building shacks and to burn for firewood. When the spring rains came, they would wash away layers of mud from the hills into the cities and villages. It was a cruel place to survive, and those who could, got out and settled elsewhere.

Lancelot Francois and Lamarrre St. Marie had found themselves a home in Fort Pierce. The city had become a haven for Haitian immigrants, so it was easy to settle in there. They had family and friends living on Avenue D, not far from the docks, and they each managed to rent a room close by. Avenue D was once the worst street in the city, home to rampant drug dealing and usage, and a never ending line of prostitutes, all willing to work for the crack they so desperately needed. But the city had cleaned it up, thanks to some Federal grants, and Avenue D had become a Haitian neighborhood. The men felt comfortable there.

Lancelot had found a job on the Nassau Queen the first week they arrived. The work on the ship was hard, but he liked the idea of being on the ocean most of the time. It was a break from the drudgery of so many hard labor jobs he had in Haiti; there, a man worked from sunrise to sunset for very little money, and he could never say there was anything left when he got done paying his bills. But here in America, he spent every day on the water, marveling at its beauty, and at the end of the week he had money left over to save. This money was going to be used to bring his wife and three children from Haiti to join him. He would have enough in the next couple of months; this kept him going every day.

Lamarre had been a cook for many years, working in hotels and restaurants around Port-au-Prince, but as the economy there turned sour, the jobs became very scarce. His last job had been as a fry cook in a Kentucky Fried Chicken restaurant. Kentucky Fried Chicken had dozens of restaurants throughout the Caribbean; some said it was the largest single chain of restaurants in all of the islands. Unfortunately, Lamarre had a grease accident, burning his right leg severely. Instead of helping him, the restaurant owner fired him for being stupid. He had often thought the owner was right; he was stupid for staying in Haiti!

He got a job working at the McDonald's on US 1, right near Seaway Drive. Two of his cousins worked there, and they had assisted him in finding work. After a few weeks, though, a position on the Nassau Queen opened up; it was a combination deck hand/cook position, and Lancelot made sure the Captain hired his friend. The two men were together on the seas; they couldn't have been happier.

Joshua Norton was a local man, born and raised in Fort Pierce. His family was part of a local legend known as the Highwaymen painters. The artists were all local black men who had been taught to paint landscapes by a prominent white artist named Bean Backus. Backus had taken a shine to his grandfather Howard and another man named Alfred Harris. Together they learned the basics of oil painting, and began to teach other black men in the area. Some of the new artists were friends, and some were family, and together they churned out hundreds of oil paintings that were sold along the local roads from the trunks of their cars.

You couldn't walk into a business, whether it was an attorney's office or a plumbing supply house, and not see one of their colorful paintings hanging on the walls. The paintings were framed in crown moldings they put together themselves, and the frames were painted white, with splashes of gold throughout. The art, once thought to be near worthless, was discovered in the late 90's and early 2000's and the prices rose meteorically. Paintings that sold for twenty-five dollars in 1975 started selling for several thousand dollars each, as collectors snapped them up wherever they could find them. His grandfather Howard, and his Uncle Robert, were two of the most talented of the early artists. Their works sold for outrageous sums; his father's brother Norman became a skilled painter in his own right and did very well selling his artwork.

Joshua, unfortunately, couldn't paint a barn with a twelve-inch brush, so he ended up working on the Nassau Queen. He was the First Mate, and he was in charge of the work load and the men. He'd made so many trips to the Bahamas over the years that he felt like the islands were his second home; one time, many years ago he had left the Queen to work on a ferry for the Albury's in Marsh Harbour, Abacos. He soon got tired of the short, tedious trips back and forth, same island to same island, over and over. When he heard the Queen was looking for a First Mate, he talked with the Captain, who didn't hesitate to hire him back. Joshua couldn't paint a barn, but he was one of the best boatmen he'd ever had on his ship.

The final crewmember was a newcomer, a local guy whose family had been around Fort Pierce for years. TW Parsons was the only white guy on the boat, but he didn't care. Like the others, he loved being on the water doing anything. He had pulled gill nets back when they were legal, and started crabbing after that. Rumor had it that he was a Square Grouper fisherman for a while, before the DEA really started hammering the local guys involved in the marijuana trade. A square grouper was a bale of marijuana sealed in plastic that was put overboard a big ship offshore, and retrieved by local fishermen. It had become the real treasure of the Treasure Coast for some time before the crackdown. It was said the grouper moved north to Brevard and Volusia Counties. The men on the Queen didn't care about his past; TW was one of them, just another brother on the water.

Captain Roland Brown was a local black man, like Joshua. His family had come to Fort Pierce before he was born to work on the farms and in the citrus groves. They were pickers mostly, and life had always been very difficult for them. His parents had six children, and he was the only boy. His father swore that his only son would do better than he ever did, and made it his life's mission to get Roland through school and into a better life. He died of cancer in Roland's last year of high school, never seeing his son walk down the aisle to get his diploma.

Roland had planned to go to the local community college after graduating, but he was heartsick over his father's death. School, for now, was out of the question, so he joined the US Coast Guard, and stayed in for eight years. When he got out he knew he wanted to be on the water, so he scored the First Mate's job on an old ferryboat, the Freeport Princess. When the Princess was lost at anchor during Hurricane Andrew in 1991, he was offered the Captain's position on a new boat, the Nassau Queen. He had now been at the helm of the Queen for seventeen years, and he had been thinking it was probably time to retire. He wanted Joshua to be his successor, the new Captain, so he had made Joshua take every Captain's course necessary to drive his boat. The young man was ready, he knew. What he didn't know was whether or not he was ready. "Time will tell, they say" he mused, as he drove the ship out into deep water.

Up on the bridge, the captain held his course. The wind had started picking up out of the southwest, but it wasn't enough to trouble his boat. While they had encountered mostly flat seas after dawn, the new wind was kicking up a three-to-four foot chop that wasn't unusual for this time of year. It was probably making it a little tougher for his crew to drink coffee, but that was certainly the worst of it.

He was right in his assessment. The splashing of sea water over the hull had forced the crew to move back off the bow, and into the small cabin they shared as a dining room and entertainment center. The entertainment was an old TV Capt. Brown had brought from home, along with a collection of DVD's nobody watched anymore. They had all seen most of the movies more than a few times, but the sound of the TV was relaxing as they sat around waiting to get into port. They were into their third pot of coffee, with The Godfather, Part II, playing on the TV, when they heard a very loud explosion on the starboard side of the ship.

The men jumped up and ran out onto the deck. There was heavy smoke coming out of what looked like a large hole in the right side of the hull; sea water seemed to be pouring into the hole, causing a loud hissing noise as the cold water hit the searing hot metal. The chop, once harmless, was slapping against the hull, driving more water in. The ship was already beginning to list to the starboard side; whatever caused the explosion was big enough to be a serious problem for the men on board.

Captain Brown came down from the bridge. "What the hell just happened? Did we get hit by something? I didn't see anything in the water, but that sure felt like a torpedo, or something like that, just hit us."

Distracted by the blast, the other men hadn't seen Joshua Norton stripping down and putting on snorkel gear. Before anyone realized it, he went over the rail into the water. The Captain and his men stood around, waiting for him to surface. When he did, his story put a chill into every one of them. "There's a horizontal tear in the hull that's probably twenty feet long by about four feet across. It's huge! It had to be explosives of some kind; the damage is beyond extensive, it's catastrophic! We're definitely going to need to get off this boat soon. There's no way it's not going under with all the weight we've got on board."

The Captain returned to the bridge and grabbed the radio. "Mayday! Mayday! Mayday! Coast Guard Station Fort Pierce, this is the Nassau Queen, out of Fort Pierce, en route to the Bahamas. We have just had an explosion in our hull that appears to be sabotage. I repeat, this is the Nassau Queen; we have had a major explosion on board that has seriously damaged the hull. We need immediate assistance; this ship is going down. There appears to be too much damage to keep her afloat. Do you copy, Fort Pierce?"

"Yes, Nassau Queen, we read you. We will send every available unit to your position asap. What are your coordinates?"

"Coast Guard Station Fort Pierce, my coordinates are 27*25'31.49"N – 79*52'26.05"W. Do you copy?"

"We copy Captain. Stay on the boat as long as you can. We'll have a helo and our big boat head your way in the next few minutes. They should be there within 15 minutes. Do you have a lifeboat on board?"

"We did, but it appears to have been blown off the boat

in the blast. It's on the same side as the explosion; I'm guessing we lost it then. My men and I have life jackets, so we can go in if necessary."

"Alright, Captain. Hang in there; we'll be there shortly. Are you carrying any chemicals or toxic materials?"

"No, I've got a boatload of sugar, if you can believe that. Who the hell would blow up a ship full of sugar? It doesn't make any sense."

CHAPTER THREE

US Coast Guard Station, Fort Pierce, Florida

Commander Rick Perry had heard the Mayday from his office. He leapt out of his chair and out onto the floor of the radio center, listening intently to the message from Capt. Brown. He knew Roland Brown personally, having met him years ago during an inspection of the Nassau Queen, and he knew that the Captain loved his ship and the men who crewed with him. He made a quick decision.

"Petty Officer, I'm flying the bird. Tell Ensign Williams to take command here for now, until we get back. That captain is a friend of mine; I want to get to him as soon as we can."

"Yes, sir, I'll forward your message to the ensign immediately. Go get'em, Commander!"

"I will, Petty Officer, you can take that to the bank!"

Commander Rick Perry had been grounded a few years back for something so bizarre it was hard to talk about. He had blown up a Coastie helo after he and two friends jumped out just before the blast, knocking the three of them into the water below like shells shot from a cannon. The fact that they all lived through the ordeal was truly a miracle, because the reason he incinerated the bird was to rid the world of a real-life demon, something he still had occasional nightmares over to this day. It all seemed like a bad dream now, but it was the scariest moment of his life, something he prayed would never happen again.

The Coast Guard issued a formal reprimand after the incident. He wasn't allowed to fly any Coast Guard helicopter or plane under any circumstances for a period of two years, and he was basically frozen in his rank as Commander of the Fort Pierce Station. What his superiors didn't know was that he loved the Fort Pierce Station; it was a terrific place to work. He had great fishing any night of the year right off the docks, and the weather was great. He suffered through the embarrassment quite well.

Together, with his old friends Captain Don Buckley and Pete Harris, he had spent countless hours chasing the big snook that roamed the docks at night. That was before the incident; the Captain had moved to the Bahamas with his wife Sue, and Pete had been killed by the monster they had buried at sea. It seemed like it was yesterday, but it had been almost four years since their nightmare. He missed Don and Pete whenever he went out on the docks to fish, but over time he had managed to move on. It hadn't been easy.

"The incident"; that's what the Coast Guard had called it, and he had accepted their terms. It could have been much worse; he had spent time in Vietnam during the war running patrol boats up the Mekong River, searching and rescuing, as they called it. Gunfire and rockets across the bow, and black body bags on deck, were everyday occurrences then, so being stuck in Fort Pierce was actually very pleasant.

But that was all behind him now; he had served his two-year suspension, and he was allowed to fly again. He still jumped at the chance to fly the search and rescue chopper that sat in his front yard, so every once in a while he took advantage of his rank and grabbed the stick of the big Sikorsky. He loved the power the helo generated and the speed at which it flew. Flying helicopters had been his dream job many years ago before he got moved along in the ranks, and it still got his juices flowing every time he flew one.

He grabbed his helmet as he flew out the door to the helo pad. The rescue crew was on board and ready to go, and the chopper was up and running. He jumped in the seat, strapped in and gave the order to take off. The Sikorsky effortlessly lifted itself off the pad and into the air as Commander Perry set a course due east, to the coordinates sent in by his friend. He saw the thirty-six foot power boat that had been confiscated from some drug runners a few years ago. With quad 200's on it, it was the fastest boat in their fleet, and now it sported the colors of the U.S. Coast Guard.

The big boat had been his friend Don's favorite when he served as the Station Chaplain, and the Captain couldn't resist taking the big blast boat out and letting it rip. Seeing the big powerboat running at full speed made him think that it was Don Buckley driving her, and not the Petty Officer at the wheel. The boat was already outside the Inlet entrance going like a bat out of hell. It was a beautiful sight!

About the Author

Mark T. Bradbury now claims the east coast of Florida as his home after almost twenty years of seacoast living. Residing on the *Treasure Coast*, named after the incredible gold and silver-laden Spanish galleons that crashed on the nearshore reefs in 1715, he's been reading and listening to the legends of the local treasure seekers since he arrived. His enthusiasm and exploration in Mayan culture, coupled with this fascination for treasure hunting, led to *Serpent's Curse*, his first novel, a combination of the two interests. He has also gone on to use the Treasure Coast as the setting for his exciting new sequel called *Serpent's Return*.

The waters of the Indian River Lagoon system and the nearby Atlantic Ocean have stoked his fishing fires since arriving here so many years ago. Bradbury feels that Florida and its waters have played a crucial role in quenching his angling interests, brought to a high point when he became involved in Coastal Angler Magazine in 2008. Publishing a local fishing magazine was just what the *Muses* ordered to ignite his writing career; he is now writing full-time and is currently working on his fifth book.

www.ingramcontent.com/pod-product-compliance
Lightning Source LLC
Chambersburg PA
CBHW061737020426
42331CB00006B/1271